T0139152

TOTALLY INTEGRATED ENTERPRISES

A Framework and Methodology for Business and Technology Improvement

TOTALLY INTEGRATED ENTERPRISES

A Framework and Methodology for Business and Technology Improvement

Thomas E. Miller • Daryle W. Berger

Raytheon Professional Services, LLC

St. Lucie Press
Boca Raton   London   New York   Washington, D.C.

Library of Congress Cataloging-in-Publication Data

Miller, Thomas E.
  Totally integrated enterprise : a framework and methodology for business and technology improvement / Thomas E. Miller, Daryle W. Berger, Raytheon Professional Services LLC.
       p. cm.
  Includes bibliographical references and index.
  ISBN 1-57444-303-8 (alk. paper)
  1. Electronic commerce. 2. Management information systems. 3. Information technology. I. Berger, Daryle W. II. Raytheon Professional Services LLC. III. Title.

HF5548.32 .M55 2001
658′.05--dc21   2001019413

Visit the CRC Press Web site at www.crcpress.com

© 2001 by Raytheon Professional Services LLC
St. Lucie Press is an imprint of CRC Press LLC

No claim to original U.S. Government works
International Standard Book Number 1-57444-303-8
Library of Congress Card Number 2001019413
Printed in the United States of America 1 2 3 4 5 6 7 8 9 0
Printed on acid-free paper

Dedication

To my father who portrays the true pioneer spirit and of whom I am very proud and in loving memory of my mother. Also to Judy, my loving wife and life-long partner who has always stood with me.

TEM

To Melvin and Jerry Berger, my parents, who taught me there are at least two sides to every story and some truth in every side.

And to Patricia, my wonderful wife, who often reminds me to not sweat the small stuff — but seldom tells me what the small stuff is.

DWB

Testimonials

Raytheon Professional Services is dedicated to helping its clients make substantial and lasting improvements in their operational and financial performance. Tom and Daryle's book, Totally Integrated Enterprises, *explains what the enterprise of the future looks like and what it takes to get there. It sets the tone for the kinds of change that RPS enables and it creates a vision of what our customers will want to be.*

Roger Blomgren,
Vice President and General Manager,
Raytheon Professional Services

The authors have packaged a complex set of ideas into an easy to understand business model. My experience with Tom Miller and the Raytheon Professional Services staff will change forever the way I approach business. This book will change the way you approach your business.

Chris Church,
Program Manager,
Compaq Computer Corporation

Having worked with Tom Miller and the Raytheon Professional Services staff, I fully endorse this unique insight on enterprise architectures that provides the framework to create value for optimizing the utilization of technology at all levels. This is certainly on the cutting-edge.

Barham Moss,
IT Services,
SBC Communications

Preface

Most enterprises, today, are in the process of reengineering themselves. Often, as a result of acquisitions and mergers, a legacy of varied cultures, resources, and processes must be reshaped into a single, integrated enterprise. Additionally, increasing pressure from global competition for narrowing markets is forcing each company to make itself a cost-effective, high-quality provider to its traditional customers while simultaneously pushing it to deploy more of its talents and strengths into new markets and product lines.

At the foundations of today's leading-edge companies is a remarkably similar vision for virtual enterprise in an agile environment where organizations can swiftly and cost-effectively move products from concept to production and respond dynamically to changes in customer and market requirements. Attributes of such agile enterprises include the ability to:

- Incorporate business strategies and functions to drive product design and manufacturing requirements, operations, and post-production activities of product distribution and support
- Rapidly integrate designers, manufacturers, and suppliers to operate as a virtual enterprise — a unified entity unconstrained by geographic distribution
- Create, staff, and empower integrated product teams, providing expertise from all shareholders, allowing timely decisions and feedback and resulting in higher-quality products in less time
- Communicate enterprise information (e.g., requirements, plans, designs, models, metrics, results, and other vital data) to and from every stakeholder in the virtual enterprise in real or near-real time
- Dynamically manage production among facilities and exchange production data and status information as a routine basis of business

Today it is recognized that the above vision and the attributes and best practices of a totally integrated enterprise are not peculiar, or exclusive, to one company. Nearly every enterprise in existence today needs to make a similar transition to a globally interdependent business paradigm.

A staggering amount of literature is available for every aspect of modern business and enterprise. Courses, classes, seminars, and experts galore are available to help you learn and implement the fine details of every value-adding, cost-saving, customer-pleasing, quality-improving, buzzword-compliant business initiative you have ever heard of, and many that you haven't.

And therein lies the rub — there is so much material, so many nuances and fine points, and so many well-qualified experts on individual topics that it becomes very easy to become overwhelmed and disoriented by it all. Studying the details of each tree doesn't really help much to navigate through the forest.

What seem to be missing in the enterprise body of knowledge are generalist documents that tie things together. The business environment today is characterized by a rapid rate of business reconfiguration, shortened periods of relevancy for expertise, higher personnel turnover, increased functional interdependency, and the pressure to include advanced technology in every aspect of business. It should not come as a surprise that more managers and leaders are being put into pivotal decision-making roles with less experience and preparation than ever before. Depth of understanding in one's technical field is clearly a strength, but a narrow focus potentially creates blind spots for lack of understanding the bigger, integrated business picture.

This book is proposed as something of a "Rosetta Stone" for dealing with enterprises, both existing and ideal ones. It provides, in simplified terms, key definitions, a comprehensive framework, and a methodology for understanding and mapping current enterprise configurations and for designing a revised architecture needed for totally integrated enterprise.

This book provides a high-level enterprise architecture that allows for the implementation of processes that facilitate the use of the best commercial practices and technologies, both existing and emergent, to improve product and process integration. It also provides a technically sound basis for the timely development and delivery of robust products, including their life-cycle support and management, within a virtual enterprise. This material, when combined with a specific enterprise mission and examples, will help form a powerful vision that creates the pull for change within an organization and presents the opportunity for change.

For seasoned managers and business leaders, this material should be something of a refresher course that helps get back to basics and helps confirm basic organizational values and direction. For the newly appointed manager, or business student, this book should serve as a primer. Understanding how it all fits together is a valuable insight for anyone involved in business today.

Acknowledgments

Many individuals have helped to shape the content and flavor of the information contained in these chapters. The authors would like to thank Levoy Hurley, Farley Palmer, and Brian Smith for their collaboration and contributions to this work.

Thanks also to Tom Austin for sharing his 30-plus years of experience and providing valuable feedback and for convincing us we had enough material to launch this book.

Much appreciation goes to our clients who have provided and will continue to provide us the opportunity to work with them and expand our understandings of their problems. Without problems there wouldn't be any appreciation for the solutions.

TEM and DWB

About the Authors

Thomas E. Miller's current position is with Raytheon as a master consultant providing leadership and technical consulting with emphasis on commercial enterprise architecture analysis and processes. He has technical responsibilities for the enterprise architecture product area and continues to create and evaluate new methodologies and processes for the competitive enterprise.

Mr. Miller has held key positions as program manager and senior scientist with Hughes Aircraft Company and as a senior scientist and senior principal with Raytheon. Prior to this Mr. Miller held positions in systems engineering and product design with Hughes Aircraft Company.

Mr. Miller has successfully led, managed, and directed projects with technical and business responsibilities. He has assembled and directed technical and management teams from the interview/selection process through to the fulfillment of the project goals. He has also performed systems engineering management directing specifications development, requirements allocation, and design and managed system design, engineering, manufacturing and testing. He has also provided enterprise level information management/technology (IM/IT) strategic planning, development and implementation consulting for the integration of business, engineering, and manufacturing information for a major automotive manufacturer. He is a former advisor for the Saudi Air Defense Command.

Mr. Miller's professional affiliations include the Data Warehousing Institute, the HTML Writers Guild, and the International Webmasters Association. He has been published in the Michigan Manufacturers Association's *Enterprise* magazine and has provided numerous presentations to the National Research Council on enterprise architectures.

Daryle W. Berger is a senior consultant for Raytheon Professional Services. He is responsible for internal product and client development, architecture and process development, and implementation planning to assist clients in achieving best-practice capabilities for competitive advantage in the global entrepreneurial arena.

He designed and implemented a global engineering notebook for an international automotive program team. He adapted MIL-STD 490A into a corporate template for specifying automotive vehicle requirements and facilitated the development and adoption of a set of vehicle integration areas for use by the North American operations of a major automotive manufacturer. He also designed, developed, and delivered several relational databases to support requirements engineering processes.

Mr. Berger led the in-country software installation team for the Malaysian Air Defense Ground Environment. In less than six months, a team of nine software developers installed, debugged, tested, and delivered over 1.4 million lines of operational software, including application, operating system, diagnostic, and support functions.

Prior to joining Raytheon, Mr. Berger was a senior systems engineer in the Ground Systems Group of Hughes Aircraft Company. In his career at Hughes, Mr. Berger provided technical, quality, and management leadership for the development and deployment of mission-critical, real-time embedded software on numerous air defense ground environment programs.

Mr. Berger holds a bachelor's degree in computer science (University of North Dakota). He also holds a bachelor's degree in education (Moorhead State University) and did graduate studies in school administration. His professional affiliations include the Society of Automotive Engineers and the Engineering Society of Detroit. Mr. Berger has been published in the Michigan Manufacturers Association's *Enterprise* magazine. In addition, Mr. Berger is a member of the Phi Beta Kappa and Phi Eta Sigma scholastic honor societies.

List of Figures

List of Tables

Contents

Chapter 1

Introduction

This book provides the foundational concepts upon which our vision of 21st-century totally integrated enterprise is predicated. It provides a framework and method for understanding and designing enterprises; it identifies best practices; and it provides a generic, high-level architecture for a totally integrated enterprise.

The purpose of this book is to provide a vision for totally integrated enterprise (TIE) and an evolutionary approach for implementing such an enterprise. The vision for TIE is predicated upon the best ideas and practices currently being used and developed among enterprises everywhere. The approach for achieving the vision starts with any current enterprise and incrementally develops it into a TIE using demonstrated, and wherever possible, commercially available capabilities and technologies.

This book acknowledges that an enterprise is more than facilities, capabilities, and technologies — enterprise is about people, too. It requires humans to create a vision for enterprise and to provide the leadership to achieve and sustain it. Only people can understand the customers' requirements, design products to satisfy them, and create and operate the manufacturing engines that deliver those products. Only people can relate and balance the myriad activities occurring simultaneously within the enterprise. Only people can learn the lessons of experience and apply them in a manner that improves the future.

Enterprise is about business. Customers directly or indirectly provide revenue that the enterprise uses to return value. The value is in the product — how it satisfies the need, how well it works, what it costs, how long it serves its purpose. An enterprise that has no satisfied customer meets a rapid demise. Enterprise is very much about using human, hardware, and software resources to perform work that provides the products (goods and services) that satisfy customers.

An enterprise is also about process. Work must be designed to achieve the purpose of the enterprise in the most efficient way. Work must be repeatable and predictable. Processes are valuable enterprise assets that must be defined, deployed, sustained, and improved. Discrete process threads, with clear inputs and outputs, are fundamental building blocks for modern enterprise.

Any type of enterprise, including governmental and military agencies, their suppliers, and nonprofit civic organizations (e.g., schools and hospitals), can benefit by including many of the best commercial practices. To that end, this book provides a framework and methodology for understanding integrated enterprise that anticipates many of the best practices and industry initiatives. A high-level enterprise architecture that incorporates best practices is also recommended. Finally, this book provides a generic strategy for implementing TIE and discusses issues associated with changing an existing enterprise into one designed to prosper in the intense environment of 21st-century enterprise.

Who Should Read This Book

This book provides information for those individuals responsible for planning, implementing, and leading an enterprise. For those who are developing enabling technology and services for enterprise, this book provides orientation and background. For enterprises that wish to become TIEs, this book provides useful insight into what changes might be needed to accomplish the task.

The primary audience for this book comprises the champions, leaders, planners, designers, and operational managers responsible for defining, implementing, and growing an enterprise. As a beginning, this book is intended to communicate a clear and consistent understanding of what is meant by totally integrated enterprise. The shared images and vocabulary that result will allow the audience to more fully address internal and external concerns from the enterprise perspective (i.e., it will be easier to put issues into the context of the big picture). In addition to provoking analyses and development of an enterprise's operational business requirements, this book also helps readers develop and implement best-practice capabilities and enabling technologies.

Readers involved in (enabling) technology development and deployment projects will derive benefit from this book. At a minimum, this book provides a context and a rationale for what they are doing. Understanding how their individual projects fit into and help accomplish the overall enterprise objectives will help to keep the projects relevant and aligned.

This book will also be useful for sharing the vision with any other enterprise that aspires to become a TIE or participate in a virtual enterprise. The ideas and concepts for best-practice enterprise explained in this book are applicable to any type of enterprise, but especially those with hard manufacturing capabilities. Because a TIE is, in almost every instance, a part of an extended, virtual enterprise, it becomes essential that any other participating enterprises also understand what is expected. If they need to make changes to evolve with the target TIE core elements, this book will serve as a reference and starting point.

Definition and Scope of Enterprise Architecture

This section provides operational definitions of enterprise and architecture as they are used in this book. A taxonomy of architecture types is used to put enterprise architecture in a context that helps define its scope of this book.

In the vast body of material about enterprise, other terms for the same ideas are sometimes used, and some of the same terms are used in different ways. Without trying to invent new buzzwords, and without suggesting that other terms and definitions are incorrect, this book strives to use the terms and definitions that are most straightforward. Terms and usage that are highly intuitive are most preferred, followed by those that seem to be most in the mainstream (i.e., those used most consistently by the highest number of references). Operational definitions, as they are used in this book, are provided both in the text and in Appendix B.

Enterprise is defined in this book as a unit of economic organization or activity; especially a business organization. A business provides goods and services to customers who need and want them. It is an economic organization in the sense that revenue is an input to the enterprise and value must be returned on that investment. An enterprise is a business organization in the fullest sense of the word. The enterprise is very much about economics and return on investment, for customers, participating organizations, and stakeholders.

Architecture is defined as the arrangement of, and interactions among, the components that comprise something. Architecture is abstract — it is not the physical components of the object under discussion. Architecture is the set of organized relationships among physical things in the static sense, and it is the set of interactions among the arranged components in the dynamic sense.

Take classic structural architecture as an example. Bricks, boards, windows, wire, and pipes are examples of physical components in a house. The architecture is captured in a set of blueprints. The architect goes through a process of turning the design-to requirements (i.e., customer wants and needs, building codes and regulations, and the science of structural engineering) into the build-to requirements (i.e., a set of architectural views that allow the constructors to acquire and assemble the components into the static structure). The architect must also anticipate how the structure will be used and what external forces the structure must withstand. An architecture that puts the kitchen and the dining room at opposite ends does not understand the dynamic flow of activities performed in the house. A roof that collapses during a severe snowstorm because a shallow, warm-weather slope was used instead of a steep slope is another example of bad architecture.

Enterprise architecture then is arrangement of, and interactions among, the components of an enterprise. The TIE architecture (remember, the E in TIE is Enterprise) is a set of blueprints that establish build-to requirements for a totally integrated enterprise that will develop, manufacture, and deliver products of choice in the 21st century.

It is possible to buy an off-the-shelf architecture for a house, and if that design happens to be satisfactory for a family's needs, then it is a reasonable thing to do. Enterprises, however, tend to be unique. Each provides a different product that it thinks best satisfies the customer. As a result, an architecting process must be performed to translate customer and business requirements into technical requirements and subsequently into an enterprise design. Similar to renovating a house, the original enterprise structure must be surveyed to determine what is still sound and what must be updated or eliminated.

Different types of architectures are used for different purposes when dealing with an enterprise. As illustrated in Figure 1.1, there is a taxonomy (i.e., orderly classification) of architecture types that is useful for understanding enterprise architecture.

A generalized, best-practice architecture (reference architecture) is used to establish a benchmark for assessing enterprise architecture. The framework underpinning the reference architecture establishes a way of looking at different enterprises in an apples-to-apples fashion so knowledge can be readily exchanged. Subsequent tailoring of the reference architecture creates the architectures needed to construct the enterprise, its business segments, and its specific product programs.

Since a reference architecture is conceptually everyone's enterprise, then specifically, it is nobody's enterprise. As illustrated, the reference architecture is created from best-practice initiatives, processes, procedures, techniques, methods, and tools from all industry types. Necessarily, the reference architecture is high-level. However, general business metrics and organizational dynamics allow for meaningful enterprise-to-enterprise comparisons and the transfer of knowledge.

The enterprise architecture provides the set of views needed to describe and relate the major elements of the enterprise (i.e., a way to look at the

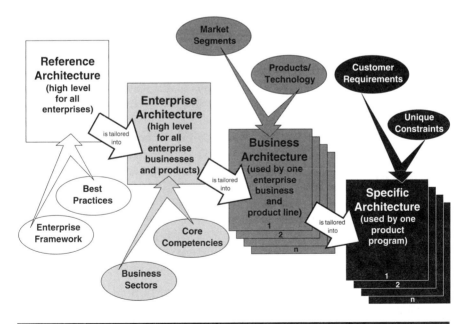

Figure 1.1 Architecture Taxonomy. The reference architecture provided in this book provides a benchmark for other enterprise architectures.

enterprise holistically). Enterprise elements, as used here, are the highest level, functionally oriented units that collectively achieve the enterprise mission. Each enterprise must define its own top-level architecture. The enterprise architecture evolves the general reference architecture into one that explicitly understands what industry sectors and core capabilities are targeted by the enterprise. Complex enterprises (those with more than one product line) also use the enterprise architecture to identify and allocate its business segments (or product lines).

Business architectures continue to make the enterprise architecture more specific. In this step, the specific market segments, and the products and technologies involved in them, are reflected in the architecture. Businesses with more than one customer also use the business architecture to identify and allocate product programs.

Product programs are usually designed for one customer or class of customers. Each customer (class) may have specific demands for the product provided by the enterprise. The final tailoring of the architecture is done to allow the product development programs to accommodate any unique requirements imposed by their customers. By contrast, the other architecture types are evolved and deployed as part of enterprise reengineering. They are reviewed periodically as a part of continuous improvement and updated as necessary to maintain competitiveness.

The scope of this book, then, focuses on the left side of the figure and provides the high-level reference architecture for a totally integrated enterprise. A generic set of enterprise elements is defined, along with a rationale for each element and some insights into how the element incorporates best enterprise practices. This book also suggests how the reference architecture can and should be applied to TIE and proposes a generic approach for implementing TIE.

About This Book

In this book is a brief overview of TIE and some of the key enablers for modern enterprise. We also reference material for understanding and designing totally integrated enterprise. Then, a set of appendices provide additional detail and reference material.

The book begins with a brief overview of TIE and how it differs from traditional enterprise. It then provides an overview of the framework and architectural constructs underlying the TIE vision. Generic best-practice notions are explained, and representative examples are used from time to time. The appendices provide additional levels of definition and detail for selected topics.

Chapter 2 examines the high-order goals of and essential capabilities needed for TIE. This big-picture view introduces the elements and structure typical of many current enterprises. It goes on to identify the five essential attributes and the advantages of each in a best-practice, totally integrated enterprise. The end objective, of course, is to evolve and integrate the current enterprise elements into a TIE. For each of the five primary attributes (goals) of TIE, the chapter describes at least one key enabler that helps realize it.

The TIE boundaries, as defined in this book, start with a core set of capabilities within a selected enterprise (the primary enterprise), for example, its administrative, engineering, research, production, and logistic facilities. The boundaries then extend to include enterprise organizations outside the primary one, for example, prime and subcontractors and suppliers. The enterprise is additionally extended to include customers as well.

Then, the book identifies a methodology for understanding and viewing enterprise architecture. Chapter 3 provides some brief analogies based on traditional (structural) architecture as an introduction to enterprise architecture. Chapter 4 introduces a model that allows for the complete and consistent examination of enterprises. Beginning with the definition of enterprise, the book ties a framework and views of an enterprise together, including business, process, and resource views. The difference between conceptual and tangible views, and core and noncore elements are discussed. The chapter concludes with a rationale for the order in which architectural views must be considered when making critical business decisions.

Chapter 5 provides a high-level enterprise architecture that incorporates a summary of the best practices and techniques currently being applied across industry. Lean, agile, total quality management, and integrated product and process development are acknowledged as integral parts of how the enterprise operates. Some affect the structure of the architecture selected; all affect the policies and practices recommended. The architecture is presented along with overviews of its four major elements: executive leadership, business development, product management, and enterprise support/enabling.

Knowing what to implement and knowing how to implement aren't always the same thing. Chapter 6 provides some insights and practical considerations about the process for evolving an existing organization into the one envisioned. An industry trend analysis is included in this chapter as a guide for what information management capabilities may be available in the next several years.

Chapter 2

Totally Integrated Enterprise

A totally integrated enterprise must be an agile, lean, virtual, learning, collaborative organization. Each essential attribute is a standing enterprise goal. Enablers are available to help today's businesses become the integrated enterprises of the future.

Totally integrated enterprise is, first of all, a vision and constant quest. Continuous improvement, as a way of life, demands that an enterprise's practices, methods, and technologies constantly change. However, the goals of TIE are robust and persistent. The goals of TIE not only anticipate changes, they depend on them to constantly signal opportunities to better align customers' needs, supplier capabilities, product designs, and manufacturing and service efficiencies. Instead of a dog-eat-dog environment, the TIE environment strives for a theme that has enterprises helping each other to satisfy consumers to ensure large, viable markets capable of sustaining everyone.

The first section of this chapter identifies five fundamental attributes of TIE that should become the overarching goals for modern enterprises seeking to play in the global markets. A definition and description for each goal are provided, along with a list of some of the most obvious and significant advantages that accrue to enterprises that achieve such behaviors and capabilities. An understanding and appreciation of these goals allow enterprise decision-makers to better assess how potential and proposed changes in the current business configuration may or may not be moving them toward the realization of totally integrated enterprise.

Each of the goals has numerous strategies and specific methods for achieving them — so many that it is impractical to try to deal with all of them. However, the balance of Chapter 2 describes, in generic terms, one key concept or capability that is essential for realizing each goal. Understanding each of these key enablers helps later in the book to understand the recommended best-practice architecture.

Totally Integrated Enterprise Goals

A 21st-century TIE will be a permanent, but continuously improving enterprise. A TIE implementation program is a series of initiatives and activities to create and implement the enabling capabilities and support functions that evolve the current enterprise into the TIE.

Presently, most enterprises are part of a complex set of individual, physically dispersed, and diverse elements. Enterprise core elements consist of any management, business, administration, engineering, production, and support capabilities and facilities owned by, or directly under the immediate command of, the enterprise. In today's business environment of specialization and globally interdependent relationships, the typical enterprise is one of a variety of enterprise chain types, each type with different roles and responsibilities, each with different business processes and rules. Moving information and material through this amalgam of separated companies is slow, difficult, and expensive. The current (extended) enterprise environment is represented in Figure 2.1.

Enterprises of the system provider type are those that provide finished products (goods and services) to the paying public. One form of system provider is sometimes referred to as an original equipment manufacturer (OEM). Automobile makers, appliance manufacturers, personal electronics manufacturers, and the like are examples. A construction company is another form of system provider — the contractor who commits to delivering a finished house to the homebuyer provides a product that is

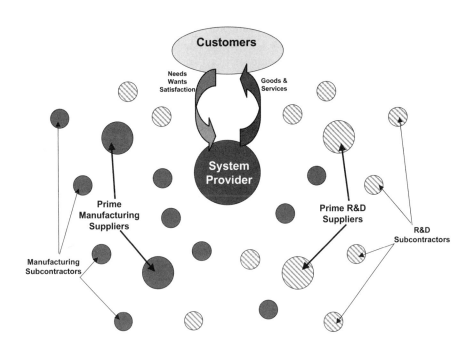

Figure 2.1   Current Enterprise Environment. The extended enterprise chain comprises numerous and disparate elements, widely separated and operating according to individual priorities and procedures.

really a system. Consulting and development firms that design and implement information systems for businesses, universities, cities, and governments are also examples of system providers.

A system provider, especially these days, is seldom capable of providing all of the parts, pieces, and capabilities needed to develop and deliver the entire system. The enterprise is extended under various contractual arrangements to include prime contractors and subcontractors who primarily provide either research and development capabilities or production capacity. For example, an automobile manufacturer (an OEM) may wish to include an all-new vehicle interior or suspension in a vehicle introduction. The OEM turns to any one of several prime contractors (called Tier One suppliers in the automotive industry) that specialize in vehicle interiors or vehicle suspensions.

The Tier One interior supplier, in turn, looks to still other subcontractor enterprises (automotive Tier Two suppliers) that specialize in materials and manufacturing techniques to help them design and manufacture new parts (panels, seats, arm rests, and head liners, for example). As the Tier

Two suppliers provide their parts or their technologies (a new plastic injection molding capability, for example), the Tier One enterprise assembles individual parts into interior modules. The interior modules are sent to the OEM's final assembly plant where they are inserted, as a single part, into the vehicle bodies moving down an assembly line.

In the current business environment, is it very easy for a subcontractor type of enterprise to think of a prime contractor as the only customer or for a prime contractor to think of the system provider as the customer. The effect of this mindset, where individual customer–client relationships are seen as the totality of an enterprise, is that parts and modules are customized and optimized for the entrepreneurial customer. Consideration for what the effect is on the overall system (product) purchased by the end user — the real customer — is often lost. Only when each customer–client relationship is seen as a link in a chain of enterprises providing an integrated product to the end buyer can totally integrated enterprise be achieved.

Figure 2.2 introduces the key attributes needed for any best-practice manufacturing enterprise. If totally integrated enterprise is the objective, as it should be for any enterprise that is part of an enterprise chain, then business processes, procedures, information, and resources must be garnered that make the enterprise: collaborative, learning, virtual, agile, and lean.

Integrated enterprise, as it is used in this document, refers to an enterprise (a unit of economic organization or activity; especially a business organization) that takes the entire customer/product life-cycle spectrum into its considerations, planning, and operations. An integrated enterprise understands its customers and how they use products (goods and services) throughout the life cycle. This end-to-end perspective allows the enterprise to factor post-production service and maintenance considerations and total ownership cost into the early stages of product conceptualization and evaluation.

Integrated enterprise also looks at all of its customers, products, and product families in a side-by-side perspective. What appears advantageous to one product program may well be disadvantageous to others. Gains in one product program may be more than offset by losses in other programs. The integrated enterprise acts for the greater good.

Clearly, what is required for integrated enterprise is a sense of balance, and balanced responses to change and opportunities that present themselves in the course of business. Balance is provided only by having a sense of purpose and direction, and by having a set of values for evaluating situations and possible responses. This center of balance that acts as the enterprise's gyroscope is a key responsibility of enterprise leadership.

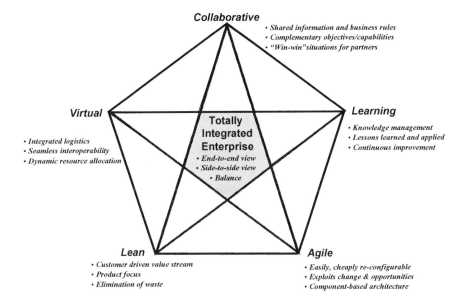

Figure 2.2 Totally Integrated Enterprise Attributes. Total integration of a state-of-the-practice enterprise, from either the internal or the extended perspective, requires that five major organizational attributes be addressed.

Collaborative enterprise refers to an organization that understands the interdependent roles of various enterprise elements (both internally and in the extended sense) and finds ways to capitalize on its collective strengths. S. Alter, in his book *Information Systems, 3rd Edition*, discusses five levels of integration between businesses and business processes: common culture, common standards, information sharing, coordination, and collaboration. The first three levels of integration allow independent processes to resolve differences, interface, and interoperate more easily — but the processes and businesses proceed according to separate goals, priorities, and decision-making rules.

Coordination creates interdependence between business elements by negotiating and exchanging control messages and by passing information back and forth in support of a common objective. However, the process for each element is still defined and executed as a unique function. Process execution attains a certain amount of integration, but any redundancies or conflicts in the independent processes remain unresolved.

Collaboration is achieved when different business elements merge all or part of their identities to accomplish larger objectives for the extended enterprise. A collaborative organization focuses on its core capabilities and establishes interlocking relationships with other organizations with different core competencies needed to achieve the end goal. To use a sports analogy, various enterprises or enterprise organizations — each one the best at its respective position — work together as a team to succeed. When the team wins, all of the players win; if the team loses, all of the players share the responsibility.

The primary advantage of collaborative enterprise, of course, is the synergy and leverage created by each team member doing what it does best. Shared objectives and mutual trust lead to faster learning and more innovation, as team members share lessons learned and create new ways to capitalize on the unique strengths of individuals.

Virtual enterprise refers to a way of doing business that transcends the physical boundaries of the elements that comprise the enterprise. Enterprise goals, processes, and operations work according to logical needs and arrangements. Many physical pieces of the enterprise, located at different sites, work together as if one.

Seamless interoperability is one of the key concepts of virtual enterprise. This suggests that compatible and common processes and standardized interfaces have been adopted. Modern information technology is also implied — shared data, integrated applications, and electronic collocation capabilities help eliminate physical limitations. Importantly, business objectives and decision-making rules are also interoperable so that the enterprise elements react to change in a similar fashion.

Real-time status and the ability to dynamically allocate resources are also part of a virtual enterprise. Scalability and survivability are attributes of best-practice virtual enterprise designs. In response to changes in the demand for, or the capability of, one or more enterprise elements, existing operations can be increased or decreased and new or replacement elements can be engaged to ensure the enterprise is operating at the necessary level of performance.

While information can be electronically exchanged at near-real-time rates among physically diverse sites, the acquisition and movement of real material and finished products must also strive for seamless interoperability. Multiple sources of material, standardized containers, and alternative methods of delivery, responsive to control pulls from the operating elements, all contribute to an enterprise capable of rapid and dynamic logistics and support.

A learning enterprise is one that understands that knowledge is power. Technical innovation, population growth, and global interdependence are all increasing at unprecedented rates. The social and economic forces that shape the markets, the materials and manufacturing methods used in modern product development, and the increasing number of international and multinational competitors constantly drive enterprises to find faster, better, and cheaper ways of doing business.

Acquiring and managing knowledge is one of the premier capabilities for best-practice enterprises. External sources of knowledge are constantly and methodically examined for change and innovation. Internal knowledge (i.e., lessons learned) is captured, shared, and reapplied among the enterprise elements. Diversity of background and cultural insights are proactively sought to better understand the customers and how products are used.

A learning enterprise also understands that change is inevitable and it welcomes change as an opportunity to improve. Continuous improvement becomes a cultural value, and best-practice enterprises build into their processes and information the ability to detect errors. Enterprise modeling is used to assess the impact of proposed changes or to understand the effect of not making changes. Metrics are designed and used to objectively measure the performance of the enterprise — both before and after changes are implemented.

Lean enterprise is predicated on the notion that everything in the enterprise should focus on the customer or class of customers and the product that satisfies them. The notion of the customer value stream is used by an enterprise to identify and eliminate waste (another common definition of lean). Activities and processes that contribute directly to the desirability of the product from the customer's perspective are said to be value adding; those that do not are defined as waste. Making an enterprise lean is about eliminating and minimizing nonvalue-adding elements.

The primary benefits of making an enterprise customer-driven and product-focused are higher-quality products, reduced costs, and shortened development and manufacturing times. Stressing customer satisfaction keeps the product on target and eliminates rework and unnecessary inclusions (scope creep). Product focus keeps bureaucratic and overhead activities from diverting resources from the value stream.

Agile enterprise refers to an organization that can quickly, easily, and inexpensively reconfigure itself to exploit an opportunity or react to change. Detecting change is part of a learning organization, but the ability to do something about change must be conscientiously designed into the enterprise elements themselves. Component-based enterprise architectures and robust components are hallmarks of best-practice agile enterprises.

An enterprise component is an element of the business, at any level, that provides an autonomous, reusable capability or function. Robust components require well-defined inputs and provide consistent outputs. The internal workings of a component are of little interest to the rest of the enterprise, but the reliability and constancy of function are of great value.

Component-based enterprise architecture depends on having robust components (functions that perform successfully in varying circumstances) and well-defined interfaces. Interface standards contribute greatly to component interoperability and reusability. They also allow for alternative components to be used to attain the same overall results within the enterprise, contributing to survivable systems and competitive pressure for lower-cost, higher-quality components. Robust components may also anticipate variable combinations of inputs and include the intelligence and flexibility to adjust to the circumstances.

The primary advantage of component-based enterprise is that the architecture can be modified easily, cheaply, and with minimal risk. Modular architectures are easily modeled, and enterprise simulations can be used to assess the impact of change prior to its actual implementation. Modular enterprises are also the ones that can take most advantage of collaboration and virtual operations.

The overall objective of any TIE implementation program is to create the enablers for a state-of-the-industry virtual enterprise and to implement them in an integrated enterprise that is collaborative, virtual, lean, agile, and learning. A TIE implementation program is a finite series of activities designed to launch the TIE. Once it is up and running the TIE, will contain the capabilities to sustain and change itself as a continuously improving organization.

Figure 2.3 represents the pentagram of best-practice enterprise attributes overlaid on the current enterprise elements, which symbolizes the objective of a TIE implementation program — namely, integration of the individual elements into a collective whole.

The integration of TIE is a total fusion of purpose, focus, risk, reward, and capabilities (including people, processes, facilities, hardware, and software). Each part of TIE must be capable of working alone, but only to the extent it provides a necessary and value-adding step in the extended enterprise. Interoperable processes and infrastructure, globally accessible information, and shared purpose result in a virtual, streamlined, cost-effective, agile enterprise that provides the best value and greatest satisfaction to the customers in the field.

Agile Enterprise

Agility is perhaps the most significant and, at the same time, the most difficult attribute to attain. The nature of change and open-ended solutions must be intentionally built into the design of enterprise components. Enterprise architectures utilizing robust components will be best positioned to exploit change as a competitive edge.

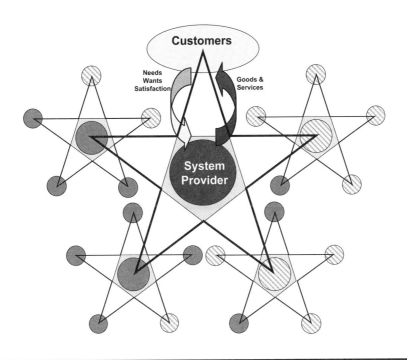

Figure 2.3   Totally Integrated Enterprise (Extended). A TIE in the 21st century must operate as a virtual enterprise — physically separate elements are electronically connected as enterprise elements collaborate to execute a unified set of priorities and procedures.

Of all the attributes needed for long-term survivability, agility is arguably the most significant. Even if your enterprise has agreed to collaborate with another, even if your information technology allows easy interoperability, even if you have the knowledge needed to make the right decision, even if your current operations are lean — all of that will be for naught if your enterprise architecture cannot be reconfigured cheaply and quickly enough to take advantage of an opportunity.

Partnerships will form and dissolve as markets present themselves and then become saturated. Information technology will continue to advance at a rate that interenterprise operations will become easier and easier. Web-based knowledge sharing and decision-making will make enterprises much smarter, and since most of the knowledge is Web-accessible, knowledge will become less of a competitive discriminator. However, experience in applying knowledge will still be a significant factor. Lean initiatives will continue to proliferate until they stop being a competitive edge and become the price of admission for playing in a particular industry or market.

Agility not only depends on a willingness to change, but also requires a conscientious decision up front to design flexibility, robustness, and adaptability into the very nature of the organization's processes, and facilities that comprise the enterprise. Point or spot solutions are replaced by set or envelop scenarios. Architectures that understand and anticipate change will not only solve yesterday's and today's problems with efficiency, they will also postulate and simulate future problems.

However, changing architectures to achieve agility is not a trivial proposition. A thorough understanding of the need for agility, and a lasting commitment to achieving it, are required by the entire enterprise, and most certainly by the leadership at the top. Agility may well be the long pull in achieving total integration. As such, the enterprise that starts to prepare for rapid reconfigurability before the need is fully on it will be the one best positioned to exploit change when, not if, it happens.

Agile, modular enterprise architecture is enabled by design and implementation of enterprise components. The following sections discuss the nature of robust enterprise components and component-based enterprise at greater length.

Robust Components for Enterprise

Change in enterprise architecture is inevitable and constant. Component-based enterprises have robust pieces of functionality (components) that can be quickly redeployed in a revised architecture.

An enterprise starts with customer, market, and shareholder voices and ends with tangible products and services in the field. A series of transforms, each converting required inputs into desired outputs, is a natural and convenient way to create order (sequence of events) and flow (movement of data and materials) within the enterprise. A component is defined as an element of enterprise that provides a unique, reusable, and scalable function. An enterprise, in this sense, is a system of interacting components.

Any enterprise system is made up of a myriad of components, some large, some small. There are special-purpose and general-purpose components, high-level and low-level components, and complex and simple components. Other components only comprise people, hardware, or software, while others include all types of resources.

Later chapters describe at greater length how components are used to architect an enterprise. This section describes the best way to identify good components and how they should behave. Well-designed, robust components (that is, components that continue to function in spite of changes or variations in their surroundings) are fundamental to integrated enterprise. Collaboration among extended enterprise entities, agility, virtual interoperability, and continuous improvement are all enabled by good components.

Components can be designated in several ways. One approach, for example, is to focus on the people who own or execute a component. Organization charts (i.e., people-oriented components) create membership sets, but they do not explain what the enterprise does to transform voices into products. People join and leave the enterprise and they reorganize themselves with alarming regularity. Strangely, or perhaps not so strangely, the same product comes out of the enterprise, regardless of the people shuffle.

Stability is one foundation for robust components. So long as an enterprise provides the same type of products to the same markets, the most stable aspect of the enterprise is the way it goes about creating and delivering the products. People come and people go, and tools they use may get better, but the fundamental nature of the work persists. Because of this, the most useful way to identify one component from another is to focus on what each component does (i.e., its function). This is the idea of process-oriented components. A process is a transform; it receives inputs, applies a value-adding function, and provides outputs.

One often-used technique for process identification and flow is the IDEF0 methodology; and its basic building-block template is useful for understanding a component. Figure 2.4 illustrates the notion. The basic block is a process, one of the framework views discussed in the following chapters. The mechanisms that enable the process are resources, another framework viewpoint. Business controls constrain or regulate the processes; i.e., the customer's requirements for the product, budget, and schedule. As will be illustrated later, this is the third aspect of the integrated enterprise framework.

A component is a physical entity. It is the sum of its resources (people, facilities, and tools), executing a defined process in support of the business and customer requirements. It has exactly the same structure as the three-view (business, resource, process) enterprise framework. To complete the IDEF0 model paradigm, it remains first to identify the input required for the component to execute its function and then to define the output of the function. This is a matter of component design, but the output is the driving consideration. Desired or required output, given the resources and constraints and the function of the component, dictates the input. The

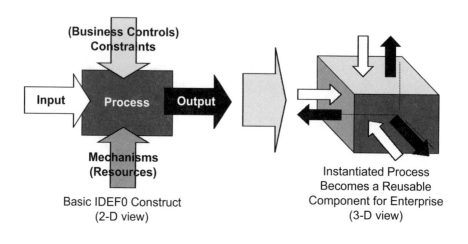

Figure 2.4 Process-Oriented Component. A component is a process (with allocated resources and constraining business requirements) that has a unique and reusable function, and that is capable of interacting with one or more other components across defined interfaces (inputs and outputs).

output creates a pull for the input. One component's input, in turn, becomes the output from other components. In this fashion, a chain of components is created that provides the product (or in other words, creates value) for the customer. The idea of a value chain is examined at greater length in a following section.

All components, regardless of their size, complexity, type, function, and composition, should exhibit a consistent set of robust characteristics or, stated differently, should demonstrate the attributes of robustness.

Components are made robust in several ways. One strategy is component cohesion. Each component performs one function or a small group of highly cohesive, operationally interdependent functions.

Another strategy is component autonomy. An autonomous component is able to execute successfully with only the inputs provided — no knowledge of other enterprise components is required.

A third strategy is component adaptability. An adaptable component anticipates different, but probable, combinations and ranges of input and has built-in intelligence to perform its function in multiple scenarios.

A fourth strategy for robust components is scalability. A scalable component has mechanisms designed into it that accommodate changes in the demand for the component. For example, a component can create a queue of task requests and work off the queue as resources become available. The queue strategy could include assessing each task priority and rearranging requests so that the most critical tasks are performed first. A component can also manage scale by accepting additional users, but slowing down the task performed for one. Components may also include strategies for dynamically requesting additional resources capable of performing the same functions and diverting the additional load to the added resources.

Robust components are valuable to agile enterprise because they are highly reusable. A component is reusable when it can be used

- As is in different executions of one process sequence
- Concurrently from different points in one process sequence
- Concurrently by two or more different process sequences

Another value for agile enterprise is provided by robust components — they can be quickly unplugged from one place in the enterprise and plugged in at another.

Component autonomy and adaptability are leveraged through formal interfaces. Formal (that is, defined and enforced) interfaces ensure that the component receives the needed inputs and assures consistent outputs. Open architecture and standardized interfaces are best practices that contribute greatly to architectural reconfiguration without destroying the functionality of the components. Open architecture also expects that a component identify itself to candidate users. This is the reverse image of formal interfaces. The component, in effect, announces, "I am capable of doing the following and if you provide me inputs in the prescribed format, I will assure you a dependable output in the following format." This, in turn, enables enterprise architects to search for internal or external existing enterprise components that satisfy business requirements to incorporate into their business structures and processes.

Formal interfaces also mean a component is able to improve its internal workings without disrupting the rest of the enterprise. The rest of the enterprise should know the component only in terms of what must be provided and what is returned. This encapsulation of the component's internal mechanisms prevents other components from establishing direct functional dependencies (pathological connections). It is this lack of direct connectivity that allows a component to be changed internally without causing unintended consequences in other components.

Component-based enterprise has several other advantages. Understanding what is required of each transform (i.e., component) defines skill requirements, knowledge requirements, and development and manufacturing requirements. Skill and knowledge requirements form the basis for personnel recruitment and development. Development and manufacturing requirements allow for the assessment and selection of tools and methods that are right for the job.

Component-based enterprise also forms the basis of enterprise simulation. Data models are used to describe the inputs, controls, constraints, and outputs for each component. Performance, cost, and quality attributes can be assigned to each component's process. Once business rules are added, enterprise simulation becomes possible, permitting what-if analysis of proactive and reactive change. This becomes a key enabler for continuous improvement and agile enterprise.

Component-based enterprise strategies are consistent with an open systems practice. Open systems have been defined as systems that are robust, modular, and adaptable to changing environments (Acquisition Reform Office, 1997 Virtual Town Hall Meeting). The open systems initiative, it was pointed out, is both a technical and business approach. As suggested previously, the technical approach of modularity and interoperability is key to adaptability and extensibility of the system. Design impact and cost of component upgrades are minimized.

As a business approach, open systems allows multiple vendors to provide system components which may be assembled into higher level systems to meet particular mission requirements. This facilitates competitive procurement of enterprise system components, implying better value.

Component-Based Enterprise

Enterprise architecture takes advantage of the principles of structured decomposition to manage scope and complexity at various levels of the enterprise. Components are discrete building blocks of functionality, arranged such that interactions among them collectively achieve the purpose of the enterprise.

At the day-to-day working level, an enterprise typically executes hundreds, perhaps thousands, of operational procedures. Attempting to deal with them all at once is clearly unworkable — so the idea of summary, or aggregate, processes are used to abstract chunks of the enterprise's work into general operations. In the same fashion, process-oriented components at one level of architecture are aggregated into a summary component in order to accommodate the architecture at another level.

One of the most difficult concepts to grasp in component-based enterprise architecture is that low-level, general-purpose components are arranged in an order (that is, they are given an architecture) to create

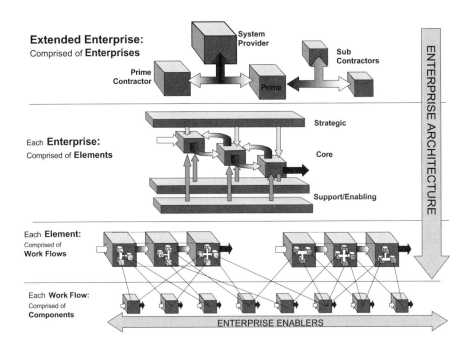

Figure 2.5 Component-Based Enterprise. Components are physical building blocks of functionality used to achieve enterprise architecture. Lower levels of architecture are used to describe the detailed arrangement of components into enterprise subsystems. Higher levels of architecture describe the integration of subsystems into the holistic enterprise system.

threads of generic functionality at the next-higher level. These generic functional threads (also called process threads) can, in turn, be interwoven with other functional threads to create a specific business element with a highly specific function. Enterprise elements are integrated into a unique enterprise. Unique enterprises are integrated into an extended, virtual enterprise. Figure 2.5 illustrates the concept.

Perhaps it is useful to use a house analogy (from traditional structural architecture) to help understand how components and architecture relate. First, consider a component as something physical that is delivered to the building site to be incorporated into the house. Bricks and boards are very simple components of the structure. Rolls of wire, junction boxes, switches, plugs, and lamp sockets are simple components of the electrical architecture. Pipes, elbows, tees, adapters, traps, sinks, toilets, and faucets are simple components of the plumbing architecture.

There are other components, delivered as a single part to the job site, that are not so simple. A refrigerator, dishwasher, or furnace, for example, from one point of view is a system of smaller components. From the house point of view, however, each is a black-box component. How it works on the inside is of no particular significance in building the house. What is of importance is its size, its shape, and what must be provided to make it work (that is, its interfaces). The dishwasher, for example, needs hot and cold clean water and electricity as inputs, and it needs a drain to accommodate the wastewater it outputs.

Now consider the architecture for a moment. How do all of the components lying on the ground magically come together and become the house of one's dreams? The architecture is delivered as a set of blueprints. They integrate the conceptualization of the customer requirements, applicable building codes, sound engineering and construction practice, and the constraints of the physical environment and infrastructure (in other words, the design-to requirements) into a set of annotated drawings (the build-to requirements) for the constructors.

Notice that the set of blueprints contains multiple architectures or architectural views. The orthogonal view of the house, in its surroundings, and the master layout of rooms are useful to the customers to understand if the end product satisfies their wants and needs, but the craftpeople who build the house have no particular use for these views.

They require the lowest-level drawings or architectural views in the package of blueprints. Surveyors and excavators use the topological view to prepare a level building site at the right location and elevation. Masons use several foundation architecture views (e.g., top, front, left, right, and rear views) to build the footings and structural foundations. Carpenters also use multiple views of the floor, wall, and roof architectures to create the structural framework of the house. Electricians and plumbers use their particular architectural views to install their particular components in a way that delivers electricity and water to the specified points in the house. This methodical series of constructive processes arranges and attaches the physical components according to the design in the blueprints or the architectural requirements.

The high-value portion of architecture is not in the individual views or in the detailed views. The value is in understanding the high-level components' intended usage and the overall arrangement and flow throughout the structure. By analogy, looking at the detailed layout of a bathroom does help to understand the house. Deciding which brand of dishwasher to buy is of little value if the kitchen has no space allocated for it.

Because lower-level architectural components use highly standardized parts, they tend to be more generic and are therefore more reusable and interchangeable. The higher-level components, by constrast and of necessity, tend to be more unique. Indeed, if an enterprise has no unique function or process, how does it maintain a competitive posture in the market? Every house has a kitchen, baths, bedrooms, etc., but how many of each and how they are arranged make one house different from the next. The appeal for prospective homebuyers is how well the overall arrangement and flow of the house will suit their needs.

In enterprise, the physical arrangement of components is seldom of interest to the customer, but the flow through the components has a significant impact on the potential buyer. The flow through an enterprise's architecture strongly influences how fast a product can be provided, how well it is made, and how much it will cost. This is the notion of the value stream discussed in the next section. Of additional interest to the enterprise, however, is how easily components can be rearranged to create a new flow to provide a new product. Robust components designed to allow new modular architecture to be realized quickly and cheaply are the best bet for agile response to shifting market and business opportunities.

Value-Based Enterprise Architecture

The arrangement of, and interactions among, components that add value to the goods and services provided to the enterprise's customers are the underlying concepts for value-based enterprise architecture.

Having good components doesn't mean an enterprise works well. The need for, and the adequacy of, any particular component can be determined only relative to the performance of the enterprise as a holistic system.

Architecture has been already defined as the arrangement of and inter-actions among the components of a system. Given the external customer requirements, environment, and constraints, and knowing the desired output — the enterprise architecture is the arrangement of enterprise components (each taking inputs and transforming them into a new output) that ultimately creates the final product. Figure 2.6 illustrates the idea of component arrangement and flow through the enterprise architecture.

Lean enterprise is predicated on optimizing those activities in the value stream (i.e., those that add value to the transformation of customer requirements into the product that delights the buyer). Elimination, or at least minimization, of waste (nonvalue-adding activities) lowers the cost of operations and overhead. Savings are used to increase product performance, decrease price for customers, and increase profitability for share-holders — if the enterprise is a for-profit entity.

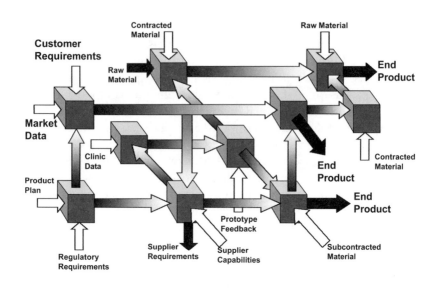

Figure 2.6 Value-Based Enterprise Architecture. Identifying which components add value in the transformation of customer requirements and market demand into end products that satisfy the customer is the basis of creating an (extended) enterprise's value stream. Such components are defined as enterprise core components.

As mentioned, the crux of lean enterprise is component optimization. Each component strives to become faster, cheaper, better. The inherent danger is that the components become so optimized, in the context of the current situation, that they are virtually destroyed when changes occur (in other words, the enterprise becomes suboptimized). If an enterprise has multiple products and market segments, a single, flexible, robust component is leaner from the enterprise perspective than multiple, equivalent components, each optimized to a single product. It is wise not to overoptimize components to the exclusion of reusability (i.e., agility). This suggests that value is determined not by each individual customer, but by the collective satisfaction of the customers for all products.

Understanding the flow (i.e., interactions) among components also contributes to enterprise simulation. The enterprise architecture defines the interoperability and interface requirements, persistent and transient data requirements, throughput rates or performance, and process sequence and timing. Coupled with the component attributes described in the previous sections and with business rules or guidance for decision making, enterprise leadership and business developers are able to analyze alternative architectures before they commit the enterprise to a new direction and business ventures.

An example of a component-based architecture is illustrated in Figure 2.7. This is not a complete architecture or a complete value stream. The figure demonstrates that an architecture integrates various types and sizes of components and internal and external flows. Any single component, by itself, does not provide any particular insight into the system or the enterprise. Each component derives purpose and relevancy only in the context of the architecture.

Virtual Enterprise Capability

Future enterprise relies on the ability of individual companies to work within one or more virtual enterprises. The ability to quickly join, participate in, and then leave the virtual enterprise's information architecture is a key enabler for agility The multicompany virtual enterprise model is an emergent best practice for information technology architectures.

Collaboration, partnerships, and mergers create multicompany virtual enterprises. Business in the 21st century will be conducted between multiple companies teaming together for mutual benefit and to meet common goals. Competitive pressures and the ever-increasing rate of change have forced businesses into relationships and interdependencies unthinkable only a few years ago. Companies will be required to reconfigure both themselves and their external relationships without disrupting the business. And they will do it often.

Portals, vortals, BI portals, B2B, and other methodologies and technologies continue to create solutions based on specific software package-to-software package paradigms. Specific areas and functional needs of the enterprise are often addressed one at a time. This look at the multicompany virtual enterprise is an option that establishes protocols of knowledge consisting of interface and data definitions/standards, which represent the core information architecture enablers for the integration of enterprises.

This leads to the selection of applications and systems that allow interoperability between companies with different systems. In this respect, each company can be viewed as an enterprise component.

Figure 2.8 illustrates a multicompany virtual enterprise. This consists of companies with different core competencies working together to create a product or service that none alone could produce.

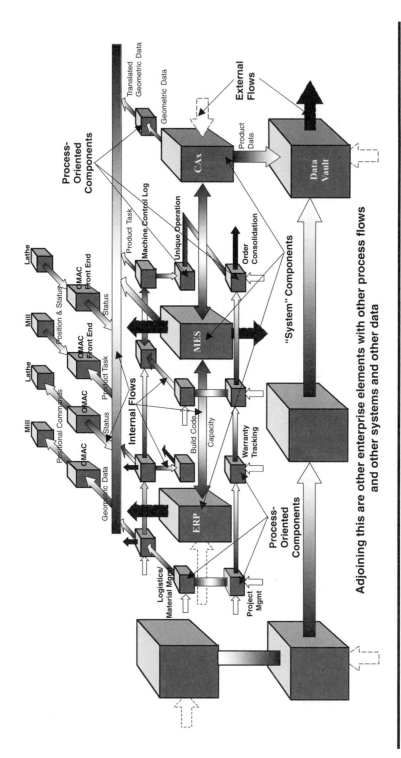

Figure 2.7 Component-Based Architecture Example. Physical components of different type, complexity, and purpose are arranged and interact to perform the work of the enterprise. In this subset of an enterprise architecture, product design data and manufacturing planning and execution control data are to Open Modular Architecture Controllers (OMAC) that manage the physical tools that shape metal.

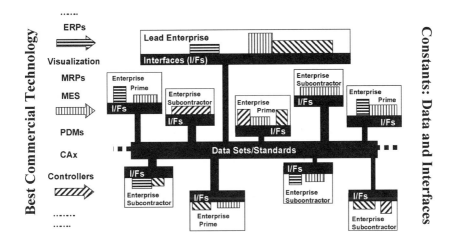

Figure 2.8 Multicompany Virtual Enterprise. This architectural option calls for protocols of knowledge consisting of interface and data definitions/standards that represent the core architecture enablers for the integration of enterprises.

This notion of virtual enterprise allows for changing the lead company, prime contractors, and subcontractors, depending on the particular product or service required. Each company with its particular core competencies may be required to be the lead at some point in a collaborative effort. This future environment will rely on new technologies that support this type of architecture.

The multicompany virtual enterprise will accomplish things its members could not accomplish individually or through traditional intercompany operating methods. The multicompany virtual enterprise also presents a whole new set of challenges. Some workers and companies will thrive, while others will resist change and wither.

Integrated Product Teams (Empowered People)

Integrated product teams (IPTs) have distinct characteristics and behaviors that require substantial modifications in an enterprise's organizational dynamics and leadership models. Changing from traditional functional organizations to IPTs is an enterprise enabler that requires special attention and resources during the cultural transition period.

IPT members represent all of the technical core and support functions and organizations that are critical to developing a product. This integrated team can match requirements and technical/cost/schedule risks against capabilities within the team and among other IPTs to optimize the end product. For this reason, IPTs should include the customer and key suppliers, because their knowledge is critical to creating the best possible strategies and decisions for meeting all of the customer's requirements. This approach to teaming differs from a traditional program organization, which was usually focused on single functional disciplines, even when teams were used.

Successful application of integrated product and process development (IPPD) rests heavily on the ability to align, empower, and lead these new cross-functional teams. High performance IPTs are enabled by a leadership environment based on mutual trust and responsibility, team and individual accountability, clearly defined goals and objectives, and decision-making at the lowest possible levels. The open environment of rapid and honest communication required by IPPD is created by transitioning from a traditional use of mandated decisions to a style of leadership that coaches and empowers.

IPTs work in a disciplined environment, and they employ consistent methods to plan, track, and measure performance and progress. The life-cycle requirements of a product must be well integrated through comprehensive up-front planning. A cross-functional team including customers and suppliers is best suited to do this planning. The IPTs must set aside time and money for this planning and resist the traditional temptation to go to work without an integrated plan. Best-practice enterprises and IPTs coordinate an integrated master plan (IMP) and integrated master schedule (IMS) to implement IPPD. The IMP/IMS relates requirements, planning, resource allocation, execution, and program tracking over the product's life. Disciplined and integrated planning ensures that teams at all levels have all information available to enhance their decision-making.

IPTs must be supported by a culture and infrastructure that integrate and align the organization in support of teams. The infrastructure should provide a method for applying resources to, and removing obstacles from, the IPTs by addressing issues and conflicts that the IPTs have been unable to resolve. In addition, it should provide a forum for timely two-way communication between the IPTs and process owners. The infrastructure should provide the management framework essential to the success of the enterprise by ensuring that team activities are integrated with business objectives. Fundamentally, the infrastructure must ensure commonality of IPPD, across multiple teams and organizations.

IPTs concentrate on the application of resources to achieve project goals; functional organizations, in turn, shift their focus to people, processes, knowledge, and technology management (development,

Key Characteristics of Integrated Product Teams

- Involve customer and suppliers early and consistently
- Produce product or service, with clear task entry/exit criteria
- Possess clear set of objectives and metrics
- Possess complete resources to ensure success
- Are a cross-functional team working toward product driven goals
- Employ integrated, concurrent decision-making
- Employ planned integration with other teams toward system goals
- Are empowered to make decisions within specific product or service goal
- Ensure good two-way communication with leadership
- Have product-related financial responsibilities and accountability
- Raise and resolve issues early
- Understand team dynamics and resolve disagreements reasonably

Figure 2.9   IPT Key Characteristics. IPTs exhibit key characteristics that integrate product, process, empowerment, collaboration, coordination, and communication.

acquisition, training, and deployment). An IPT consists of empowered members, that is, people who are qualified to do the work and are able to speak and act for their organization(s). They are authorized to make binding decisions and commitments on behalf of the organization they represent. IPT members are accountable for the eventual success or failure of the entire product, not just their individual contributions.

IPTs have key characteristics that clarify their roles and responsibilities as identified in Figure 2.9.

Collaborative Enterprise

Of all the attributes needed for totally integrated enterprise, collaboration is the one that requires no specialized technology, yet it is one that is probably the hardest to obtain. A new spirit of leadership that requires openness, trust, and

> mutual respect for all participating organizations is required. This substantial change in the business culture represents the greatest challenge to enterprise leadership today.

Collaboration, frequently defined as a shared-creation-for-value enterprise, yields a net product from the multiple companies (or business areas within a distributed company) that comprise a virtual enterprise. The partners in a collaborative enterprise must adopt a mutually compatible set of processes that create a valuable product or service — valuable to the market that buys its and valuable for each partner in the enterprise. The following are key enablers:

- Establishment of shared goals
- Support and endorsement of executive leadership
- Management cooperation and coordination
- Establishment of shared operational rules

Within a proposed virtual enterprise, shared goals serve as an arbiter in determining the shape, the settings, and the communication requirements. The establishment of shared goals enables the multiple areas or businesses to define the key deliverables produced by the collective enterprise. These deliverables are used to establish a framework for attaching the shared operational rules. Defining these shared goals is the responsibility of executive leadership. Endorsement by the management level provides a cooperative coordinating environment that enforces the shared operational rules.

These concepts preempt any discussion of technology. Technology may be chosen to support collaboration and is certainly used for communication, but without these enablers, technology alone provides mediocre performance improvements. Collaborative enterprises focus on trying to create a rhythm, a tempo, and a flow of communication that prevents them from interfering with one another while assuring that events are proceeding toward the accomplishment of the goal.

Establishment of shared goals defines the product or services that are to be produced in terms of requirements. These are the requirements for profit, design, manufacturing, implementation, and so forth. There must be a shared understanding of these requirements to enable a common product or service focus.

Executive leadership support and endorsement are required to form a binding agreement among the different areas or businesses that comprise the enterprise. This often becomes bogged down in discussions with lawyers and contract personnel and can look like a brick wall. Executive leadership must break down the brick wall and work through the different agendas to enable contracting without undo constraints. Executives' strategies will be the cues for their management teams.

Management cooperation and coordination among the different areas or businesses will provide for team building and the definition of the shared operational rules. This is not so much an enabler as it is a way of maintaining a teaming relationship with the different areas or businesses that comprise the enterprise.

The establishment of shared operational rules is like creating a playbook for a sports team. It defines how the plays will be executed and the particular roles that different team members will perform. You can see that without this playbook games would be won only by extraordinary performance by individuals. If those individuals get hurt or leave, the term confusion would be the word of the day.

As mentioned earlier, collaboration happens both simultaneously and asynchronously. A virtual enterprise needs to have rules that share and leverage each participant's core competencies for reaching the goal, but at the same time let each participant respond to changes in a prescribed manner. Stated differently, shared rules let the businesses make compatible course changes when confronted with obstacles in the path of the normal mode of operations.

Chapter 3

Introduction to Enterprise Architecture

Enterprise architecture can be a complicated subject. It has, however, strong parallels with traditional architecture. Everybody lives in some type of housing, and whether they realize it or not, they instinctively understand some basic principles of architecture.

This chapter is about understanding and creating enterprise architecture. That sounds like a simple enough proposition, but the inherent complexity in both enterprise (a unit of economic organization or activity — especially a business organization) and architecture (the arrangement of, and interactions among, the components of a system — in this case, an enterprise) make for a complicated task.

As a simple way to start thinking about enterprise architecture, we need only think about the houses we have lived in, live in now, or would like to live in in the future. The sections in this chapter use familiar situations about houses and remodeling to introduce the need for architectures, the nature of architectures, and the value of being able to envision the integrated architecture before the cost and effort of physical construction are incurred.

Terminology in any discussion is always an issue. This book uses words and terms in specific ways. Definitions are provided both upon initial usage and in Appendix B. Other definitions of the same words are possible and, if assumed, may create confusion.

Need for Enterprise Architecture

Restructuring an enterprise is a difficult task at best, and a downright risky venture if the current and planned enterprise architectures are not well understood. Corporate mergers, divestitures, and continuous improvement dictate frequent enterprise remodeling. A whimsical analogy with traditional architecture helps to underscore the need.

Let's begin with some fun. Imagine, if you will, that you have come into a substantial sum of money. You won the state lottery, or some rich, but unknown relative left you an inheritance — you may have some other favorite fantasy, but pretend you have acquired a large enough chunk of change to really impact your lifestyle.

Imagine, too, that old house next to yours, the one with the great room with the magnificent fireplace and the built-in, wood-paneled library that you've always admired, has just come onto the market. Now let your imagination really run wild and start thinking about the possibility of buying the house next door and creating a new mansion out of the two existing houses.

How to join the houses … let's see? A circular drive up to a covered entrance with art galleries leading to either side … or perhaps a work-out area with a lap pool running between the houses … and maybe an atrium or indoor greenhouse … or … well, you get the idea. The possibilities seem endless and they are all exciting.

You find the seller's agent and buy the house before the opportunity slips away. Then you call your contractor brother-in-law (well, really he is a great mason, but has lots of experience and buddies to give him advice) and tell him what you have in mind. Those of you who have ever done any remodeling, or have watched any of the popular television shows about home repair and reconstruction, have probably guessed that this is about where the fun stops.

That big shrub against the facing wall was removed only to uncover the well. Well? Oh well, it is an old house. How much could it cost to cap a well and hook into the city's water system? Besides, your brother-in-law loves to work with a rented backhoe.

The call you get from your brother-in-law the next day is not the highlight of your day. It seems that in digging trenches for the water line and the footings for the connecting structure, he found not only the TV and phone cables, but the underground electrical main for the neighborhood. Good news, your brother-in-law suffered only a minor shock. The neighbors, on the other hand, aren't so happy. Oh, and you may want to call your lawyer ... something about an easement and whether you want to defend against the utility companies jointly or individually.

The utility companies weren't totally unreasonable. Since you are paying for repairing the lines, for a little bit more, they agreed to reroute the cables behind the old house, instead of between the houses. Of course, that meant digging up the septic field (I told you, it's an old house). Besides, how much can it cost to hook up to the city's sewage system?

After the infrastructure issues are sorted out, you go on to learn even more about your new old house — the one that used to be a blacksmith's shop. No wonder the great room was so great and the fireplace was so big. Cleaning up the buried slag pit was almost free, considering you had to rip out the septic field anyway, but the environmental report was unexpectedly pricey. The wall you had planned to knock down turns out to be solid brick. It was the outside wall of the shop, but was covered over in wood paneling to make it seem like an interior wall during the first remodeling.

The old copper wires are in fine shape, but they are undersized by modern standards. You have two choices — leave the four outlets exactly as they are and where they are (which means you can't put in the home entertainment system you have in mind) or completely replace the entire electrical system and bring it up to modern codes.

The silliness could go on and on. But needless to say, there was a fatal omission in our whimsical approach to merging domiciles. How much grief could have been avoided if the city plat book had been consulted to see where the houses were located relative to water and power, and where construction would be restricted by easements? How much easier would it have been to decide whether the old house was the gem that it seemed, or was even capable of being converted into your dream house, if blueprints (for both the original shop and the remodeled house) were available?

By now, it should be obvious that understanding architecture and having blueprints are absolutely necessary to plan and execute any kind of structural change.

How is merging two enterprises really any different than joining two houses? Have you really done due diligence if infrastructure issues (physical, cultural, and informational) were not researched and evaluated? Do you think the cost of infrastructure changes is any less expensive, relatively speaking, in business than in housing? Does it seem unreasonable that existing enterprises were built to old standards, and they become as-is constraints on your new business or additional expenses to update?

While you may not think of asking your brother-in-law to come in and remodel your business, how is that really different from asking technology vendors and enterprise service providers to turn your business in the enterprise of your dreams? If you think that's possible, just imagine inviting the very best electrician, plumber, carpenter, and mason you know out your house. Tell them they have three months and half a million dollars to create a state-of-the-art house.

Now imagine coming back in three months. What are the odds you are going to feel really good about how your money was spent? How much better would you feel if you had spent some time and money with an architect who could provide the blueprints for the home of your dreams to the contractors of your choosing?

Nature of Enterprise Architecture

An enterprise's architecture requires multiple architectural perspectives, each with a different aspect and purpose. Complexity is introduced when the individual architectures must be integrated and balanced into a holistic enterprise. An analogy is provided to assist in understanding these complexities.

Imagine a group of friends standing in front of a building being asked to describe the entire building, its contents, and what the occupants do in the building, but each person gets to look through only one window. One person looks through a window and sees a group of people eating at a table. Another person looking through a second window and sees shelves full of books and a person studying at a desk. A third person looks through a different window and sees somebody asleep in a bed. The fourth friend looks through yet another window to see small children playing in a room full of toys and games.

When the group convenes to report its findings, the first person announces that the building is a restaurant. The second person scoffs and says the building is a library. The third person expresses disbelief, saying the building is obviously a hotel. The fourth person declares all of his ex-friends as crazy, revealing that the building is a childcare center.

The conundrum is that every person is correct in what he or she saw, but each is wrong about what the building really is — a typical four-bedroom home. Guests are enjoying a gourmet meal in the dining room; the children, having eaten earlier, are playing in the nursery; the teenager in the den is doing homework; and the person asleep in one of the bedrooms works a night shift.

The fallacy (and the moral) of the story is that it is impossible to look through one window and understand an entire building, its arrangement, its contents, its occupants, and its usage.

To understand the house and its goings-on, many different but complementary views are needed. For example, lifting the roof off and looking down from the top reveals the number and arrangement of the rooms. This is a more complete view, but what about the contents? How do the occupants use the rooms and what is in them? How would the occupants like to use the rooms? How are water and electricity distributed throughout the house? How are heating, cooling, and ventilation provided? How about the views when looking out of the windows — where are the neighboring houses? Do the terrain and landscape around the house create drainage problems, obstructed views, or steep grades for the drive and sidewalk to the street?

It is obvious that describing the architecture and activities of a house is not as simple as it might seem. Now imagine trying to describe a complex manufacturing enterprise that has multiple products, employees and facilities located in numerous places, and customers in every corner of the globe. Looking at just the manufacturing or marketing or distribution aspect of a business is no different than looking through one window. Worrying about optimizing the payroll system or the travel policy or getting the cheapest computers is no different than changing the layout of a house to shorten the plumbing to save money. The house may well have the cheapest plumbing, but if the flow and functionality of the house are lost, who will buy?

Not only is the description of architecture complicated, so is the process for creating an architecture. An architect creates a book of plans — he or she provides many different views of the house, each with a different aspect. But there is a method and an order in creating the various views. For instance, the plan for the plumbing or wiring is not created first, simply because the house needs water and electricity.

The architect begins by sitting down with the family and learning how they intend to use a house and what features in a home are most important to them. The experienced architect asks about initial cost, operating costs, and maintenance. The architect also is aware of building codes, standards, and regulations and discusses these constraints with the clients. All these elements together comprise the system requirements.

After gaining insight into what the house is intended to be (for the family), the architect begins with conceptual views. The house is illustrated in its surroundings. Proposed views of the outside and of the important features of the inside are prepared and presented to the family. After these visions of the house are confirmed, the architecture begins the task of creating the technical views of the house for the builders and contractors who will collaborate in preparing the lot, constructing the house, and connecting the house to the existing infrastructure (streets, water mains, power lines, etc.).

While developing the technical views, the architect finds that achieving one objective (for example, lots of glass to enjoy the view from the family room) conflicts with another (economical heating and cooling) because the family room faces south and gets maximum exposure to the sun. The architect, concerned with pleasing the customer, involves the family in the discussion and suggests compromises. The family, understanding the conflict, provides guidance so that the house still provides the most satisfaction for the money they are willing to spend.

The experienced architect, knowing that families grow and change, also prepares several alternative visions for the house after several years of use. The house is designed in such a fashion that it does not prevent modification at a later date.

During construction, the builders and contractors find variations in the lot or materials that require adjustments in the plan. They also suggest changes to make things easier, cheaper, or better. The architect, understanding the family's desires, negotiates with the builder to accommodate changes that improve the house's quality or price without sacrificing the family's needs.

Just as the architect requires a set of plans for a house, this book presents many different views of an enterprise. At times it may seem confusing; but the reader needs to avoid the temptation to look through only one window. Enterprise architecture is, at first, a complicated subject to understand; as a result, patient and persistent reading of this book may be required.

Just as the architecture has a rigorous method for leading a family through the process of dreaming, drawing, and building a house, this book presents a method for consistently using market and technology opportunities to evaluate and decide the need for change. The next section discusses the major views of enterprise needed to specify its architecture. The section also provides insight into the proper order of events needed for sound architecture that serves the need of the whole enterprise.

Integrated Enterprise Architecture

People and tools are becoming available to help business leaders and managers envision and evaluate their current enterprise architecture and its impact on operational effectiveness. In the future, enterprise simulators will be able to help predict the outcome of internal changes and different external stimuli.

The problem with a set of blueprints is that each page (while providing distinct, value-adding information) needs to be mentally interleaved, or integrated, into one conceptual image. Not only does the architect need to be skilled in creating blueprints, but the contractors and builders responsible for physically building or altering the structure must also be skilled in reading and interpreting blueprints. Two-dimensional conventions must be melded into a real-world image of the finished house.

Not only is it necessary to see the static view of the house just sitting there, but it is essential to start imagining how the house stands up over time and usage. Foreseeable weather conditions should be imagined to assess how well the house maintains its integrity. Typical family events and happenings should be imagined to judge if the house makes it easy or difficult to do the most frequent and important tasks. Economic projections can be examined to see if the house will maintain its value and is commensurate with its neighborhood.

Imagining enterprise architecture is even more difficult than imagining a house and its use. First of all, there are typically more perspectives to consider. Then, too, the typical enterprise has multiple products and product organizations, so it is really a set of similar, but not quite identical (sub) enterprises. Third, enterprises tend to have different products in varying stages of development and production at any point in time, so there is a need to integrate different processes and programs into a common timeframe. Finally, there is a need to integrate across conflicting interests and priorities from within the enterprise's operations. Well-intended suggestions to make one process easier, or one product line more profitable, can have unintended consequences in the larger enterprise context if the total effect of change is not understood.

Similarly, an enterprise must look ahead and see what the competitive environment may be and assess how well it can weather change. Economic trends must be anticipated to make the enterprise profitable over the longer term. An enterprise needs to maintain its capabilities to keep up with the competition, but must also be careful not to overbuild capability in an industry or market that is unwilling to pay for the extras.

Just as there are architects to help design and build homes, there are enterprise architects emerging to help companies do remodeling. Sometimes called enterprise engineers, these are people with broad and long business backgrounds, who most typically started in a technical arena. These are people who by experience have been exposed to multiple products, programs, and client environments and who (by training or instinct) have come to see the relationships and interactions among the many moving pieces of the enterprise machine.

In addition to people to help with the integration of enterprise architecture, there is an emerging breed of tools designed to help understand how the parts of an enterprise fit together and, more importantly, how the enterprise behaves in response to various controls and stimuli. Today, prospective customers are able to sit down at an automobile dealership, specify a model, color, and options, and then see the exterior and interior of their dream car from multiple perspectives.

Similarly, there are software tools to help envision enterprise. Numerous virtual manufacturing systems are available that provide the capability to design a potential factory, insert tooling, lines, and operators, and then see how the factory actually operates. Spatial relationships and conflicts can be examined and resolved. Line rates can be varied to see how well potential choke points appear.

Enterprise flight simulators are being developed that model the cultural, technical, and economic behavior of an enterprise. The algorithms for organizational and quality behavior are still in a state of development, but forward-thinking enterprises may well choose to become involved in the development activity and allow themselves to be modeled as part of the validation activity. Not only will such enterprises be on the inside track to influence the capability of the tools, but they will also have a head start in the cultural adjustments it will require inside the enterprise to openly describe the group dynamic and to trust the model's recommended changes.

Chapter 4

Methodology for Understanding Enterprises

A method for looking at and evaluating enterprise architecture is needed to know if it is complete and adequate. This chapter identifies essential aspects of enterprise architecture and explains key concepts for a totally integrated enterprise.

This chapter more fully explains how enterprise and architecture are used in this book. It provides some general concepts and heuristics about enterprises, frameworks, architectures, processes, and enterprise components in order to illustrate many of the conclusions and guidelines that influence the rest of the document.

If the reader is familiar with enterprise theory, this chapter should be familiar. For the uninitiated reader, this chapter provides simplified notions for dealing with the complicated realities of enterprise structure and dynamics. Understanding the terminology as used in this chapter is basic to understanding the generalized and specific discussions about enterprise architecture in the chapters that follow.

Enterprise Definition

The concept of enterprise is based on a broad definition that comprehends the strategic direction, the business rationale, the internal processes, and the support functions and enablers needed to provide value-adding products and services to the customer.

Webster's Dictionary provides several definitions for enterprise. "An undertaking that is especially difficult, complicated, or risky" certainly seems to apply to today's competitive manufacturing environment. But the most appropriate definition of enterprise is as a unit of economic organization or activity; especially a business organization.

To be a viable business, an enterprise must create some unique value to customers — causing them to engage that specific enterprise. This is the ultimate criterion by which any enterprise is measured. Does the enterprise create and deliver something to its customer(s) that is worth paying the price asked? This is not a matter of profitability: even nonprofit enterprises must provide adequate value to customers for the money spent or the customers will find alternative courses of action. If profit is a requirement of the business, then some of the savings that are realized by removing cost and improving enterprise efficiency must be returned to the stockholders. If the enterprise is nonprofit, then the savings can be shared with the customer in the form of lower price, increased performance, or a combination of the two.

If providing superior value to the customer is the impetus behind business, then knowing the customer becomes critical to success. The obvious and ultimate customer is the one that buys a finished product. However, the enterprise that delivers the end product typically requires inputs from other businesses that provide the material, parts, subassemblies, and shipping material. Still other businesses may provide services for design, research, testing, delivery, or service of the product. In this case, the final product provider becomes the customer to many other enterprises. But the money the system provider needs to pay its suppliers must come from the end customer, hence the notion of a value chain. The end manufacturer and all its suppliers have a vested interest in satisfied end customers.

The chain of enterprises that collectively delivers a product to the end consumer is often referred to as an extended enterprise. As illustrated in Figure 4.1, individual enterprises vary in size; and they are contextual.

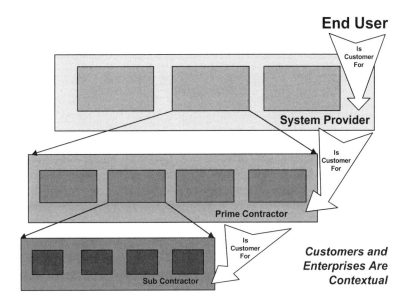

Figure 4.1 Extended Enterprise Chain. One enterprise may be a part of another enterprise, but the functions of all enterprises are essentially the same. Lessons learned in one enterprise can be applied to another, even though the output and scale are different, according to the needs of the customers.

One person's enterprise is a supplier in the next person's enterprise. While each enterprise is different in the specific scope and content of its products, the functions of each enterprise are fundamentally the same. Each has at least one immediate customer and superior value must be provided. And in a value chain, all the enterprises share the end customer. This commonality of function and purpose is fundamental to the idea of studying enterprises generically and being able to apply the lessons learned by one business to others.

The ability to create a unique value to customers is also referred to as a competitive or corporate advantage. The advantage is in two parts: as suggested earlier, the enterprise that best understands the customer is in a superior position to deliver a product that absolutely delights the customer. Knowing the right product, however, does not mean that the enterprise can deliver it. The other part of the advantage is to have an enterprise that is capable of executing the design, delivery, and support of the product. To devise this portion of the corporate advantage, enterprise leaders and planners need a comprehensive framework for understanding the enterprise in all its aspects. Such a framework, based on industry best practices, is provided in the next section.

Framework for Integrated Enterprise

Every enterprise has many facets; but for the sake of simplifying the task of viewing, assessing, and comparing (disparate) enterprises, a framework with four dominant reference planes is adequate for describing enterprise architectures.

Framework has two commonly used definitions in discussions about enterprise. One notion is that framework is a foundational or primitive structure; that is, the beginnings of the architecture itself. It is analogous to the foundations and frame structure of a house just beginning construction. Depending on its design (for example, the load-bearing walls for a house) the framework bounds and constrains any subsequent architecture and potential future changes. The second definition, and the one used in this section, thinks of framework as a reference, or coordinate, system for describing (all) architectures — it is not the rudimentary architecture itself.

By analogy, a set of blueprints describes the architecture of a structure (e.g., a family home, a church, a manufacturing plant). Each page is a different view of the structure: top view, side view, electrical wiring, plumbing, etc. Each view is necessary, but shows only a part of the architecture. The framework, by contrast, provides a set of criteria by which it can be determined whether a set of blueprints is complete and consistent. The architectures of the church and house can be compared meaningfully because they both rest on the same reference grid established by the framework. In spite of physical differences, best practices and lessons learned can be transferred from one building's architecture to another's because the framework provides a common intent.

Two different enterprise models are combined to form the enterprise framework. The triangular model illustrated in Figure 4.2 is a variant of a very common pyramid model used to portray the strategic cap of any enterprise. For the purposes of defining an enterprise-wide umbrella of strategic direction, only the first four levels of the pyramid are needed: vision, values, mission, goals. Objectives and strategies derive from and align to the overall mission and goals, but as will be seen later in Chapter 5, they are tailored to reflect specific areas of responsibility within the enterprise.

An enterprise vision is a clearly communicated image of what the enterprise looks like and how it behaves in its ideal state. Vision is something that needs to be shared by the executive leadership with

Figure 4.2 Generic Enterprise Strategy Model. The strategic direction of the enterprise, as set by executive leadership, drives all elements of the enterprise toward a shared sense of purpose.

everyone in, and associated with, the enterprise. Values guide and influence enterprise behavior. When faced with dilemmas and decisions, values provide the guidelines for how the enterprise should act. Values determine which enterprise behaviors are rewarded and which are discouraged. The enterprise mission states what the enterprise does and how that creates value for customers, stakeholders, and the community. Goals are long-term achievements or accomplishments toward which the enterprise constantly strives.

While vision, values, mission, and goals are persistent, long-term ideals of leadership (not quite ever reached) objectives are near-term targets for enterprise performance. In light of the vision, mission, and goals, executive leadership must translate the intangibles into specific expectations. Objectives are quantifiable, and progress toward them can be measured. Objectives should ask for reach, but attainable objectives are required to prevent the enterprise from dismissing them as unrealistic and therefore requiring no effort.

Strategies are known methods, techniques, processes, and procedures that are selected to make the enterprise move toward its objectives, and thus goals, mission, etc. Strategies are used to plan and execute the work of the enterprise. Progress against the work plan can be used to monitor and predict the likelihood of meeting the objectives in the time and budget allocated.

The second model used in the enterprise framework is a cubic model featuring the three major aspects of enterprise already identified: business, resources, and processes. Raytheon, as an example, uses a cubic model to align business programs and functional organizations, and they add (and emphasize) process as another reference plane, see Figure 4.3.

The multidimensional model provides several key tenets for understanding an enterprise and creating a framework for examining it. First, an enterprise is a system — it has many parts and the net effect of the interactions among the parts is what must be kept in perspective. Enterprise must be viewed holistically, and decisions and strategies must be balanced in the best interest of the entire enterprise system. Second, there are three basic aspects of enterprise: business areas, resources, and processes. All aspects of the enterprise, however, must be aligned to a strategic vision and mission for the enterprise. Finally, every enterprise must devise strategies for competitive advantage that reflect the sum of all enterprise elements and interactions.

The notion of a cubic model for viewing enterprises has its origins in another well-established organizational model, the matrix organization. Functional blocks of talent and resources perform similar types of work

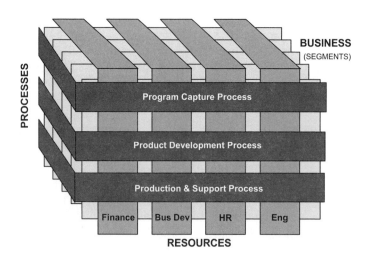

Figure 4.3   Raytheon Model for Enterprise Alignment. The Raytheon model shows how common processes can be shared across different business segments and executed by cross-functional teams.

across multiple business or product programs. In the framework, the people, facilities, and tools provided by traditional functional organizations are referred to as the resources. The various product lines and business contracts being executed for customers are referred to as the business units or segments.

A more recent notion in organizational dynamics and performance emphasizes processes as an intellectual asset and as a means for making an enterprise ever more efficient. Having a customer (i.e., business) is critical; and having the people, tools, and facilities (resources) to make a product is essential; but knowing how to do the work, in what order, and with the least amount of effort is what makes one enterprise more effective than others. This is the primary determinant in why one business succeeds where others may not. Repeatability, predictability, learning, and improvement are possible only when processes are known, practiced, and continuously enhanced. The process aspect of the enterprise creates the third dimension of the enterprise cube model.

The Raytheon cube concept and a pyramidal (3D) version of the leadership triangle are used to create a generic set of reference points (i.e., a framework) for viewing any enterprise. Figure 4.4 illustrates the concept.

One key concept of the framework is that each high-level reference point stresses different questions in a set of questions that needs to be answered continuously in the course of conducting the enterprise's work.

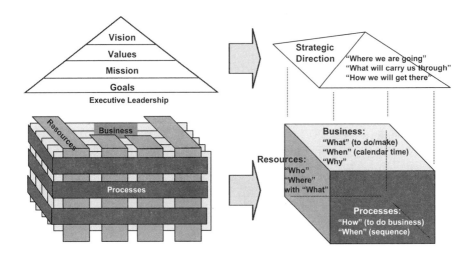

Figure 4.4   Integrated Enterprise Framework. The integrated enterprise framework looks at enterprises through four different filters — strategic direction, business, resources, and processes.

Figure 4.4 also introduces the interrogatives addressed by each reference plane. The next section discusses the views within the enterprise framework at greater length.

Enterprise Views

Enterprises are complex entities whose contents require multiple pictures or views to understand. A means of identifying and orienting the views (each with a different emphasis) and a means of relating one view to the others are provided by the framework.

A case for needing more than four planes to view an enterprise could be easily made. However, the enterprise framework provided here has at least one virtue in that it attempts to keep things as simple as possible. The house of the enterprise, suggested by the graphic in Figure 4.5, is direct and intuitive. Although simplistic, the framework is, by definition, inclusive — even though some elements may be a forced fit, the framework is of little value if it is incomplete.

Expansion of the four dominant viewpoints provides insight and criteria by which to arrange and orient the many different initiatives and tools currently being offered to improve enterprise. If something seems to be missing from the framework, it is probably an issue of semantics or the fact that the framework in its basic form is so abstract and at such at high level. Later chapters provide additional details and insight into the content of the views. The objective here is simply to identify the necessary views and rationalize them.

As mentioned in the previous section, each reference plane stresses different enterprise interrogatives — the who, what, where, when, why, and how of enterprise. The emphasis on some questions does not exclude the other questions; it simply suggests that one view may be easier to use depending on the question. It is also important to remember that all questions must be answered simultaneously and that all views act as constraints on the others. The trick, of course, is to keep all of the issues in balance and make decisions that do the most good for the enterprise as a whole.

The executive leadership point of view deals with the questions of strategic direction: Where are we going? What will carry us through? How will we get to where we want? This view is monolithic and

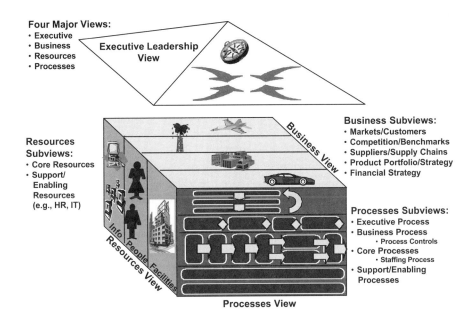

Figure 4.5   Enterprise Views. Each point of view in the framework emphasizes a different set of objects and information in the enterprise but does not exclude the other views — the same enterprise is behind each reference point.

pervades the entire enterprise. The compass and arrows in the figure symbolize the direction and coordination of movement expected from the enterprise's highest level of leadership. All activities and organizations in the enterprise must somehow align to and sustain the overarching leadership view.

The business view addresses the questions: What should we make? Why? When (calendar time) does the market or customer need it? This view, as explained in the next section, is unique in that these questions can be answered only by asking outside the enterprise. The marketplace and potential customers are the source of the information needed to make the business decisions — business is not a matter of internal invention and an advertising push at unsuspecting customers.

The process view of enterprise addresses two primary questions: How is the work to be performed? When (sequence) are tasks to be performed?

The resources view of enterprise deals with the following questions: Who does the work? Where is the work to be performed? What tools and facilities are to be used to do the work?

The primary reason for creating separate views is that each set of questions can be answered independently of the other views, at least initially. The enterprise cannot fully function until all questions are answered, but it is important to answer each question based on best-practice and independent criteria and then trade off the ideal answers into a balanced whole. For example, it is critical that the question of what to do or how to do work is not answered by explaining the capabilities of who is going to do it. "Because the tools are there" is not a good answer for why a product should be made. Trying to answer all of the questions from a single viewpoint is like trying to explain what an entire house and its contents are by looking through a single window. It seldom provides a complete and accurate answer.

Each view of the enterprise (other than executive leadership) has some primary segmentation based on the differences between market segments and/or core competencies and support/enabling functions. Core competencies are processes and resources that provide the unique quality of the product or service that the customer values and that make one enterprise different from another in the same market. Core processes and resources must be owned by the enterprise. If someone else owns the process or the resource, then by definition it is not unique or core. If one enterprise can buy the process or resource, so can another. Support or enabling processes and resources may be owned, but in many cases it is more cost-effective to buy a supplier's core competency and use it. The framework comprehends the (minimum) set of views, listed in Table 4.1, as the ones needed to examine and compare enterprises, at least at the higher level.

Table 4.1   List of Enterprise Views

Enterprise View	*Dominant Focus*
Executive management view	Strategic direction; priorities; balance
Business view	Market analysis; product concept; development program launch; customer satisfaction
Resources view	Unique capabilities; IPPD execution
Core Resources:	Integrated product teams
(People, facilities, tools)	Prerequisite capabilities; scales of
Enabler/support resources:	economy; nondifferentiators
(People, facilities, tools)	
Processes view	Value stream; common process;
Executive leadership	synergy; continuous learning
Business development	(including: corporate knowledge,
Core competencies	lessons learned, and research)
Enabler/support processes	

Business View of Enterprise

The business plane of the framework connects potential buyers with the products and services they want (in the context of competition and supplier availability). Only in this way can the economics of the enterprise be understood. Although having excellent processes and resources are necessary, there is no enterprise without the ability to generate revenue, return on investment, and superior or innovative products.

The business view is the one that comprehends customers and markets. Therefore, it is the only view capable of suggesting products and sales potential with a mind to revenues and return on investment. Since providing goods and services to customers is the enterprise reason for being, the business view is the dominant view when decisions must be made to trade resources or process development against satisfied customers; see Figure 4.6.

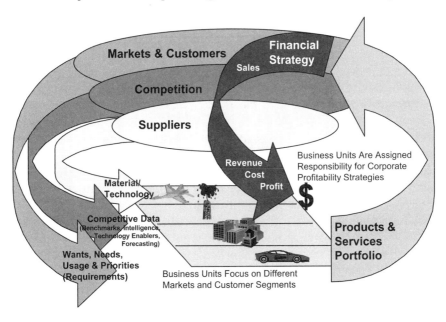

Figure 4.6   Business View of Enterprise. The business view is the dominant view of enterprise because it is the only one that can drive the enterprise to respond to customers and the competitive environment.

One significant aspect of the business perspective is the need or desire for a product. The business view must answer: Who is out there? What do they need?, and What are they willing to spend? Best-practice enterprises constantly seek information from customers and potential customers. Listening and responding to complaints and suggestions are keys to having enthusiastic customers that buy again and sell others. Market intelligence is a premier asset for any enterprise — certainly for an agile one.

The next issue the business view addresses is whether or not there is any room for new or increased competition. If other suppliers can satisfy the demand before an enterprise can develop and deliver a new product, then it is as if there is no demand. The business view must understand who else is trying to satisfy the customers and how well they are doing it? If other suppliers are not satisfying customers, then a market opportunity exists — if the enterprise can provide better value for the dissatisfied market.

The third issue for the business view is whether the enterprise has, or can realistically acquire, the capability (including the capability of accessible suppliers) to satisfy the customers in the perceived market. Objectivity and pragmatism are essential characteristics for the enterprise leaders and business decision-makers who answer this question. A golden market opportunity and a bold product vision are for naught if the enterprise really does not have, or cannot acquire, the knowledge, skills, and capabilities to execute a successful product development program. A product that does not meet its performance objectives or is late to market or overruns the budgeted cost often becomes an economic liability and a source of embarrassment in the marketplace.

One of the key notions for viewing capability is the extended enterprise. Not owning all the necessary capability does not mean an enterprise must stop pursuing a product program. Collaborative enterprise is predicated on the idea that a group of enterprises, each with complementary capabilities, can quickly and easily band together into a virtual, extended enterprise. Knowledge about suppliers and their capabilities and aspirations is another vital piece of business intelligence. Partnerships are formed around product programs. Relationships are formed and dissolved according to the needs of the customer and the product demanded. It is entirely possible to be collaborating and competing with the same partner on two different product programs. This business environment requires agile thinking and a way of creating win–win business scenarios.

Finally, there is the matter of predicting how well a product or service, delivered at a projected price, will sell and perform against the competition — this is the basis of the business case. If a market, a product concept, and the ability to produce the product exists, there is still one significant issue. The business view ultimately must create some reasonable expectation that if the enterprise chooses to launch a product program, the investment can be justified, that is, there is a return on investment (ROI). The business view is ultimately a financial view; sound fiscal practice and clear economic strategies are essential.

It should be emphasized that sound fiscal practice and ROI are not the same as profits. Not-for-profit enterprises are every bit as concerned about ROI as for-profit enterprises. ROI, as used here, means providing superior products (goods and services) at the lowest possible costs. Colleges and universities, publicly funded civic organizations (like hospitals, libraries, museums, theaters, etc.), government agencies, and the armed services all understand that they must provide as much bang for the buck as is possible. Indeed, because these organizations cannot hide inefficiencies behind dividends paid to stockholders, the nonprofit enterprises have even greater incentive to be at the leading edge of industry practice in order to ensure continued interest, confidence, and investment from those who provide revenue through taxes and contributions.

Process View of Enterprise

The process view addresses which activities add value for the customer and products. Process standards establish how well the necessary work is being performed and become the basis for repeatability and continuous improvement.

The process plane of the enterprise framework identifies the work to be done. Stated differently, it describes how to achieve the business and product goals. A customer-centric enterprise puts the customer at its center and all other enterprise activities are evaluated relative to how well they contribute to overall customer satisfaction. See Figure 4.7.

A different paradigm, but one with identical results, is the idea of a demand stream. If the ultimate goal or demand of enterprise is a satisfied customer, then the vision of a customer — happy with the product over its useful life and ready to buy again — creates a pull for all enterprise activities that supply that result. Every enterprise component is viewed either as a tributary that feeds the stream of customer satisfaction or as a wasteful function that needs to be eliminated.

Not every facet of enterprise has a direct impact on the product or customer. If value is added directly, the activity is said to be in the value

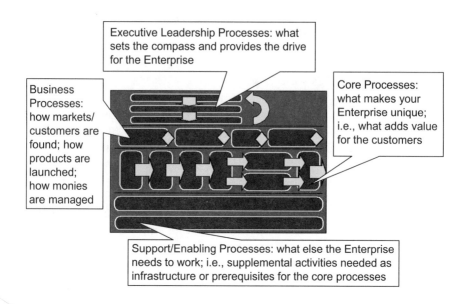

Executive Leadership Processes: what sets the compass and provides the drive for the Enterprise

Business Processes: how markets/ customers are found; how products are launched; how monies are managed

Core Processes: what makes your Enterprise unique; i.e., what adds value for the customers

Support/Enabling Processes: what else the Enterprise needs to work; i.e., supplemental activities needed as infrastructure or prerequisites for the core processes

Figure 4.7   Process View of Enterprise. Every activity in the enterprise is a process that should be documented and reviewed to align and balance the activities for optimal performance at the enterprise level — process mapping facilitates interoperability and seamless interfaces.

stream. By definition, any activity in the value stream becomes part of a core process. To the extent an activity enables or supports core activities, every enterprise component can be deemed as adding value for the enterprise or not, even though it is not a core activity. Excessive costs incurred by noncore activities, when included as overhead in the product price, diminish the value of the product in the customer's estimation. This is why so many vertical enterprises are outsourcing noncore activities and creating an interdependent, extended, virtual enterprise.

The process plane is also the view for structuring methodology (i.e., how work is to be done) and enabling tools and techniques. Process is defined as a series of actions or operations conducing to an end. The idea of describing how to achieve what is desired is vital to any enterprise. One-size-fits-all, off-the-shelf tools and vendor techniques do not define processes. Commercial off-the-shelf (COTS) tools are cost-effective solutions when they are intelligently evaluated against the needs of the enterprise's business and processes and selected because they provide an answer. However, buying an off-the-shelf solution to a unique, but undefined, enterprise problem seldom provides the payback promised and has caused many hopeful enterprises much grief.

Documented processes become a powerful enterprise asset that

- aid training and knowledge transfer
- provide repeatability and predictability — important to certification
- provide metrics that aid project management and the computation of earned value
- provide the basis of continuous improvement

Process models, as an extension of the business models, are also an important piece for creating an enterprise simulation capability.

Core processes are proprietary capabilities that provide unique product and service attributes, which in turn, appeal to customers and allow the enterprise to compete successfully. To have a competitive advantage, an enterprise needs the ability to provide at least one product aspect that it makes better, cheaper, faster, more convenient, more prestigious, more something-of-value to the customer than the competitor's. An enterprise may have a unique technology or tool that makes it special, but more times than not, the difference in competing enterprises is a matter of which one has the better processes.

Support and enabling processes may be proprietary, but they may also be thought of as a commodity that can be obtained from outside sources. Outsourcing of noncore activities is currently a widely practiced means of streamlining enterprises and lowering operating costs. The argument is that another enterprise practicing its core activities should be more efficient than one providing a secondary activity as the price of doing business. Scales of economy can be gained by sharing the expense for nondifferentiating services with others, including the competition.

An agile enterprise, and certainly an extended enterprise, relies heavily on services and (sub)products being provided by outside suppliers. However, great caution must be exercised to ensure that what was once a unique source of satisfaction to the customer is not lost in the effort to optimize cost. If a process or service that gives the customer value is transferred to another enterprise, then an enterprise has simply invited its customers to eliminate the middleman.

Resources View of Enterprise

The resources view of the enterprise framework deals with the issues of who does the work, where the work is performed, and what tools are to be used. The effectiveness and efficiency of resources management can be measured only from the perspective of how well the enterprise processes are executed to satisfy the business requirements.

The resources plane of the enterprise is comprised of people, tools, and facilities. These are usually organized by functions that align with areas of expertise. These organizations are usually referred to as functional organizations or are said to contain functional expertise. They may be financial, business, engineering, manufacturing, logistics, information services, legal, facilities/plants, etc.

The integrated enterprise views the functional organizations more as homerooms for resources and less as performing organizations. The functional organizations are responsible for acquiring and caring for the resources needed by the enterprise's business areas and processes. These resources are shared to optimize the enterprise.

Best-practice enterprises regard personnel as their premier resource. They seek, recruit, employ, nurture, and motivate personnel to provide the attitudes and aptitudes needed by the enterprise. Agile, learning enterprises change constantly. As a result, the knowledge, skills, and talents needed in the work force must be constantly aligned with changing needs of the products and the processes that produce them. Fiefdoms of expert knowledge, protected at all costs, give way to collaborative, learning organizations willing to share knowledge. Learning organizations reeducate themselves when needed by the enterprise.

Tools, as used in this framework, are force multipliers. They are elements of hardware, software, and basic techniques that allow work to be done more effectively and efficiently. Tools are selected because they satisfy the process and business requirements placed on them. Tools are enablers; they influence, but do not define, the enterprise's business or processes.

Work needs a place to be done. Organizations acquire, operate, and improve facilities and plants needed by the enterprise processes and personnel. Facilities and plants, in a sense, are a special form of tools for people and processes. As with other tools, personnel must be educated about facilities and have confidence they are adequate for the job.

Resources (people, facilities, and tools) are categorized as core or noncore. Core resources are those that execute the core processes that make the enterprise what it is and different from its competitors. Core resources are what deliver unique value for the customers. Core resources must be owned by the enterprise as proprietary assets. Noncore resources are those that support and enable the enterprise, but are not what directly provides value for the individual customers. Noncore resources may be owned, may be provided by extended enterprise partners, or may be procured from outside agencies.

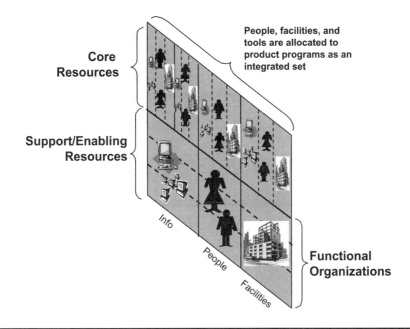

Figure 4.8 Resources View of Enterprise. In an integrated enterprise, functional organizations are not performing organizations — they are centers of expertise that provide repositories of people, facilities, and tools that are allocated/shared over the spectrum of business programs for maximum benefit to the enterprise.

The resources available to an enterprise must be balanced across the enterprise activities according to the business strategies, see Figure 4.8. Giving all the best resources to one critical program may be appropriate for an enterprise's survival. However, agile enterprises typically provide each program with a blend of experience and capability levels. This ensures every program has a cadre of experienced resources and increases the performance of the whole enterprise.

Agile enterprises also allocate resources as integrated enterprise components. Teams of people, already familiar with their facilities and tools, and performing processes they have done before, contribute significantly to reduced development times and high first-time product quality.

Architectural Progression

The order in which enterprise architectures are examined is not an arbitrary or whimsical matter when analyzing the potential impact of change. Failure to perform a complete and methodical architectural analysis often results in changes with less than expected results and occasionally disastrous, unintended consequences.

Not all views of architecture are created equal. Lower-level, or domain-specific, architectures inherit the limitations and boundaries imposed by the higher-order architectures. A simple analogy makes the point. It doesn't seem plausible that the first drawing done for the house will be the electrical wiring diagram. Imagine an electrician handing the architect his drawing and saying in effect, "Here's the ideal way to wire the house, so just build some rooms and stuff around what I gave you."

Yet that is often what happens in enterprise today. There is much innovation in business. Skilled technologists sit down with an enterprise and create bold and imaginative answers to that enterprise's problems. And then something insidious happens: the solution for one enterprise is suddenly seen as the solution for all other enterprises. The temptation to just buy the magic answer often overwhelms common sense.

By definition, core competencies are created and executed so that each enterprise has a unique value for the market. The operative word is unique, as in one-of-a-kind. If another enterprise has the answer to your problem, you don't have a business, at least not for long. If your business is unique, then how can the answer to the other person's problem be the right one for you? The process that is used to find and solve a problem can be the same; in fact, in this case it is highly desirable. Proven methods with solid results should always be sought. Similarly, the people and tools used to develop an effective answer should be reused. But the idea of buying someone else's solution, hoping against all reality that it will fit your (unique) problem, doesn't seem logical on the face of it.

As such, others' successes, and the introduction of new technology, present opportunities for change in your own enterprise. The similarities among enterprises allow for lessons learned to be applied to each, although in a tailored fashion. Benchmarking and technology studies will frequently provide ample opportunity to visit your enterprise architecture to see if it can be improved.

The fundamental axiom in evaluating change and its potential impact on enterprise architecture is that all architectural views are revisited, starting from the top. Figure 4.9 illustrates the order in which the various aspects of enterprise architecture should be evaluated, regardless of where the initial proposal for change thinks the change should be made. Often, the higher-level architectures do not have to be modified to accommodate a change at the technology or domain level. However, an assumption that

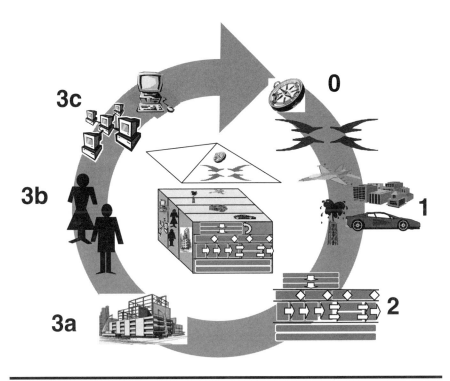

Figure 4.9 Enterprise Architecture Progression. Opportunities for change and improvement should be walked through the entire set of enterprise architectures to ensure a complete impact analysis and a balanced decision about change.

a low-level change will have no ripple effect on the overall operation of an enterprise has been the source of a costly blunder more than it should.

The enterprise strategic direction should be checked first for continued alignment. Most technology changes don't really affect strategy, but every now and then something like the Internet comes along and represents a fundamental shift in business paradigms that do require new missions, goals, and objectives. It's worth asking, but not too much time should be spent philosophizing.

The first architecture that needs to be examined in detail is the business architecture. The business architecture is the only architecture that can really decide if the change in enterprise architecture will be worthwhile in terms of profit or value returned on the investment. Quite often proposed changes are rejected out of hand because nobody makes the business case. The assumption that there is not enough money often stifles innovative and cost-effective ideas. If the change diverts money in the short term, but then gives all that back and more, then doesn't it make good business sense to proceed with the improvement?

The second architecture to be examined is the process architecture. Changes in technology typically imply changes in how the work is being performed. Shortcuts often aren't. Fancy tools require additional skills and training for those who must use them. Additional skills that require new recruitment or substantial retraining of current employees can introduce a cost that more than offsets the cost savings in technology or time. Changes in business architecture will almost always call for some restructuring of the processes that achieve the business requirements.

The business requirements and process requirements, in turn, drive the evolution of the physical enterprise (i.e., the resources architecture). If the business and process architectures represent the problems to be solved, then the resources architectures are the solutions. The first resource to be examined should be the physical plant and facilities architecture. The reason for this is that this architecture is the hardest, slowest, and most expensive to change and provides the heaviest constraints on the design of the solution. Minimized change here speeds up implementation and lowers effort.

The second resource architecture to be considered is the human resource. People are more easily changed and moved about than buildings and capital equipment, but often resistance and cultural inertia need to be overcome. Once the attitudinal barriers are removed, there are still the time and cost of education and skills development to consider. Compounding the redesign of the human resource are the issues of compensation, recognition, rewards, and so on that must typically accompany changes in job classifications. The human resource provides the second stickiest wicket in the change process.

The final architecture to consider is the information resource architecture. Information and information technology are inherently modular and adaptable. More bang for the buck is available every year, quarter, month, and day. Of all the architectures most capable of integrating and working around the constraints of the other architectures, it's the information architecture.

Of course, this is why there is all the hoopla about enterprise integration. The common misperception is that enterprise integration is an information and information technology initiative. It's not! It is the logical conclusion to an otherwise thorough and methodical architecting process that identifies and implements improvements in enterprise. Although it is often tempting to cut to the chase and talk IT, the number of enterprises that have done just that and then expressed a great deal of unhappiness and dissatisfaction should be caution enough. However, upon reflection, it should not be at all surprising that failure is the result of ignoring architectural progression.

Federal Enterprise Architecture Framework

The U.S. government has recognized the importance of establishing a uniform manner of specifying and deploying information technology through federal offices. To this end, it has created its own enterprise architecture framework.

While still in the chapter about enterprise framework, it is appropriate to briefly mention an emergent information technology framework that will likely receive increasing attention over the next few years, especially among companies doing business with the federal government — the Federal Enterprise Architecture Framework. Executive Order 13011, Federal Information Technology, established the Chief Information Officers (CIO) Council. The Clinger–Cohen Act of 1996 assigned the CIOs with the responsibility to develop information technology architectures (ITAs). This Federal Enterprise Architecture Framework (Federal Enterprise), created under the guidance of the CIOs, is used to promote shared development for common federal processes, interoperability, and sharing of information among the agencies of the federal government and other governmental entities.

This reference document also deals with the different facets of an enterprise architecture and framework. The Federal Enterprise Architecture Framework is adaptable and recommended for use in federal government wide efforts, Multi-federal agency (i.e., two or more agencies) efforts, and whenever federal business areas and substantial federal investments are involved with international, state, or local governments

Figure 4.10, however, illustrates a significant concern with the federal architecture. When looking at the federal architecture on the left side of Figure 4.10, the top of the pyramid starts with business architecture, and correctly so. The pyramid has been used in numerous models and illustrations for years. The concern with the pyramid model is that whatever is at the top looks significantly less important than the base simply because of the area allocated to each tier.

The business architecture (and its supporting business processes) carries significantly more importance than the Federal Enterprise Architecture Framework potentially implies. Relative to its significance and level of effort, it can be argued that the inverted pyramid on the right side of Figure 4.10 would be the better model.

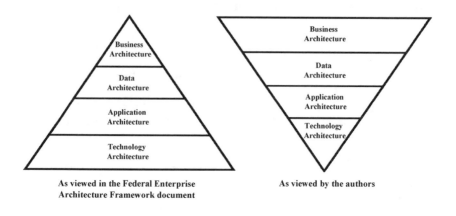

Figure 4.10   Perspective on Importance. The business architecture or business rules should carry significantly more importance than the Federal Enterprise Architecture Framework portrays.

Simply stated: business requirements drive data requirements that drive application and systems development. The lack of a good way to portray an enterprise framework is one of the reasons the house of enterprise illustrations contained in this book were developed.

The Federal Enterprise also fails to discuss value in terms of lean and agile in significant tone to allow the reader to understand their significance.

The Federal Enterprise Architecture Framework document provides some excellent perspectives. We have included the introduction and its vision as Appendix H of this book. Currently, the entire document may be obtained at the following Web site:

www.itpolicy.gsa.gov/mke/archplus/fedarchhtml/feaf_1-1.htm

Chapter 5

Best-Practice Enterprise Architecture

A generalized, high-level enterprise architecture provides a standard by which existing enterprises can be measured and from which enterprise improvements can be planned. An architecture of enterprise elements is provided that is derived from best commercial practices for enterprise.

In this chapter, framework takes on its second meaning — that is, the framework provided in the following sections is the recommended rudimentary architecture for a best-practice enterprise. The foundations provided assume that the enterprise

- Is distributed geographically among owned and allied facilities
- Must operate as a single organism
- Is sensitive to changes in the environment and responds quickly
- Is customer-oriented
- Avoids waste

Enterprise architecture is the arrangement of enterprise components and the interactions among them. As explained in the previous chapter, an enterprise component is an autonomous, reusable business function (i.e., process), including the methods, people, and tools required. As a result, the architecture descriptions that follow have a strong bias toward the process view.

The process perspective, however, is ideal for a generalized, best-practice architecture. Focusing on how each component should work provides the basis for long-term, robust requirements for engineering and implementing an enterprise. The day-to-day particulars of how and with what each component is executed are details that follow the high-level architecture provided in this document. Moreover, as technology and practice advance, the details of execution are continuously improved, but the general concept of how the component fits within the enterprise remains stable.

Accordingly, each section in this chapter emphasizes high-level functions or processes as the structural elements of the architecture. General strategies for achieving the functions are provided, along with the advantages and disadvantages, if appropriate, of doing so. Critical inputs and prerequisite events for processes are explained. The identification and suggested arrangement or sequence of processes are derived from generic, commercial best practices. References to best-practice methods, techniques, skills, and tools for implementing and executing the components' functions are provided; but the level of detail needed to fully explore each individual option's strengths and weaknesses must be part of a continuation book.

High-Level Architecture

The high-level enterprise architecture identifies four fundamental elements that provide the most basic processes for enterprise: executive leadership, business development, product management, and enterprise support.

At the highest level, the enterprise architecture consists of four large elements: executive leadership, business development, product management, and enterprise support. As suggested by Figure 5.1, each element has a fundamental purpose, performed by a distinct enterprise component or group of components. Executive management and business planning and operations are primarily enterprise planning components. The integrated product teams are the primary operational components that

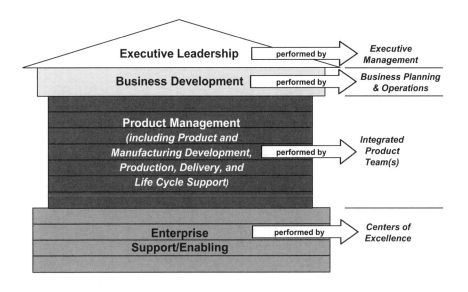

Figure 5.1   Enterprise Architecture Elements. Four elements of the physical enterprise perform the fundamental enterprise processes and comprise the rudimentary architecture (framework) of the enterprise.

develop, produce, and deliver the enterprise's products and then support them in the field. The centers of excellence components are enterprise-wide sources of enabling support.

Figure 5.2 is the same house of enterprise shown in Figure 5.1, except that it is shown in three dimensions. This perspective allows several major observations to be made about each of the four architecture elements.

The roof over the enterprise is the executive leadership element. It is enterprise-wide; at the top of the roof, it is also enterprise-common. The enterprise vision, the guiding values, the overall mission, and the goals of the collective enterprise are shared by all enterprise components. These are the elements of leadership that create the culture and establish mutual aspirations and trust among the various parts of an enterprise. As specific goals and strategies for achieving them are set by the leadership, some delineation and tailoring are required to ensure that the specific needs of each major market and business segment are directly addressed. Each business segment is aligned with the higher-level goals but focused on a different set of customers. The next section provides additional discussion of the executive leadership element.

The business development element is enterprise-wide when viewed from the processes perspective. The overall activities, business rules, and decision gates used to find market opportunities and launch product

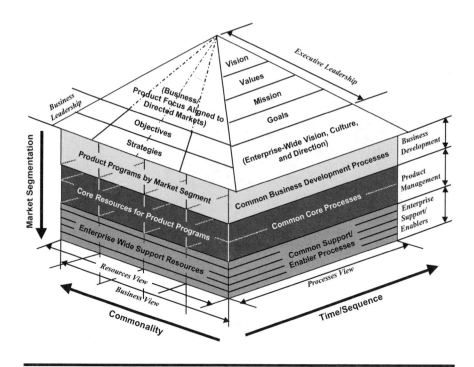

Figure 5.2 Aspects of Enterprise Architecture. When viewed from the processes, business, and resources perspectives, additional insight is gained for each of the four major architecture elements.

programs to exploit them are shared across various market segments. From the business and resources perspectives, a complementary set of business development components are created, according to the specific knowledge and expertise required to address the different market and customer needs and the products that satisfy them. It is these differences in market and product line that drive the variation in goals and strategies mentioned in the previous paragraph. The business development element is explained further in the business development section.

The product management element is actually a group of enterprise components. Most of the components are integrated product teams (IPT) executing one or more specific product development contracts in an integrated product and process development (IPPD) environment. There is another component, however, that is orthogonal to the individual product development activities which coordinates the product concepts and technologies among the product lines and also transfers knowledge (lessons learned) from one product program to those that follow. The product management element, along with IPTs, IPPD, and the required core competencies for product development, are discussed in greater detail in the product management section.

From the processes perspective, the activities, business rules, and decision gates for integrated product development are shared as much as possible across programs. From the business perspective, each IPT aligns to one business development component. To the extent that product knowledge is unique, then from the resources view, unique resources (especially people) are aligned to the business component. However, for discipline-based knowledge (e.g., electronic circuit design, noise and vibration, or thermal dynamics), enterprise-wide resources are allocated uniformly across the various product programs.

The enterprise support element is also a group of enterprise components. Centers of excellence are components that are enterprise-wide from all perspectives. They are support/enablers. The processes for each of the support/enablers are common across all segments of the enterprise. The support/enabler component resources (people, facilities, and tools) are shared by the other enterprise components at all levels. The enterprise support/enabling section identifies six key best-practice centers of excellence and provides an overview of each as an enterprise component.

It should be noted, however, that centers (as used in this discussion) are virtual centers. While it may be appropriate to support a distributed enterprise from a single physical location, the emphasis here is on having a collaborative, virtual repository for expert knowledge, lessons learned, and common process. The distributed elements of a center can act as a unified capability for the rest of the enterprise by utilizing the infrastructure for integrated information sharing.

As stated earlier, the best-practice enterprise architecture is process-oriented. Figure 5.3 provides a process framework overlaid on the four major architecture elements illustrated in Figure 5.1. Appendix E provides a Process Classification Framework for Generic Enterprise, created by the American Productivity and Quality Council (AP&QC). The best-practice architecture is derived in part from the AP&QC framework, particularly the list of support/enabling components.

The sections that follow provide additional detail for each of the processes shown in Figure 5.3 and the enterprise components that execute them. Each of the discussions is generic, and the ideas and practices can be applied to any enterprise. In order to be truly useable, however, each enterprise must examine and tailor the processes and components into ones that make sense for the specifics of the enterprise, its markets, its products, and its customers.

Figure 5.4 exemplifies how one enterprise fit these elements into its architecture. Notice the executive leadership piece at the top. Under it is the business development processes. The IPPD segment includes two core processes (competencies): program management and product and manufacturing development. The underpinning support/enablers, while stacked

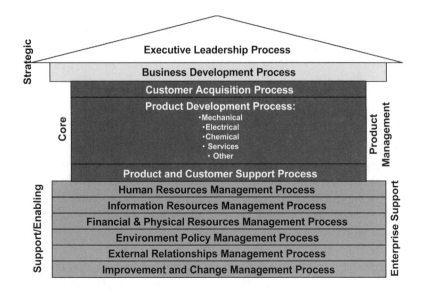

Figure 5.3   Enterprise Process Framework. The high-level, best-practice enterprise architecture is oriented around components that execute the enterprise-level processes shown.

vertically in the process framework, are organized horizontally across the bottom of this model.

Executive Leadership

Executive management continually performs the executive leadership process to determine the direction and well-being of the enterprise.

As illustrated in Figure 5.5, executive management is responsible for four primary areas of executive leadership: leadership, strategic direction, deployment and execution, and results. The four strategy areas listed under strategic direction are common to most enterprises. Depending on the enterprise, there may be other strategy areas that are just as important and should be evaluated as well.

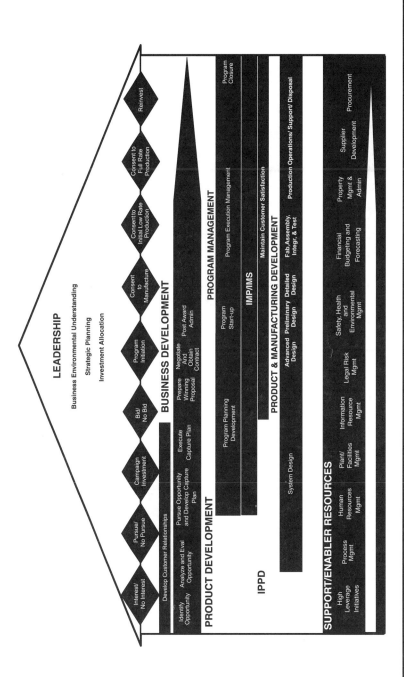

Figure 5.4 Integrated Enterprise Example. An enterprise can combine multiple views of the framework into a single picture to represent its architecture. In this example, key enterprise processes are overlaid on the enterprise elements.

Figure 5.5   Executive Leadership Model. Four primary strategies are continuously examined and refined by the enterprise leadership in order to create and maintain a competitive advantage.

The following are the types of questions required to derive deployment and execution processes for each strategic direction area (shown in Figure 5.5):

- Customers: What are the enterprise's markets, customers, and product strategies for winning? This strategy must answer the question, To achieve customer satisfaction, how should the enterprise appear to its customers? Customers is used as the label to emphasize their importance.
- Process: What is the enterprise's operational strategy for winning? This strategy must answer the question, To achieve and sustain competitive advantage, at what business processes must the enterprise excel?
- People: What is the enterprise's people strategy for winning? This strategy must answer the question, To have a winning team, what competencies and behaviors must the enterprise master and stimulate?
- Shareholder: What is the enterprise's strategy for increasing shareholder value? This strategy must answer the question, To increase shareholder value, how should the enterprise appear to its shareholders?

Not only does the executive leadership set the strategic direction, but also they champion and proactively oversee the deployment and execution of the vision and policies they put into place. It is imperative that leadership be visible to the organization and that they demonstrate the values and behaviors they ask of the enterprise. Leadership must also be readily accessible to address issues and remove obstacles that arise as the organization implements the (new) vision, strategies and processes.

As Figure 5.5 illustrates, the leadership process is a continuous activity. Each area needs to be revisited at a specific interval (once a year, for example) to maintain a competitive position. As the executive leadership practices its cycle of continuous improvement, it also sets the example for the entire enterprise.

Business Development

Business development is an enterprise-spanning group of activities concerned with obtaining markets and customers, and developing and sustaining the required business cases. Data gathering and information assimilation are critical in supporting this process.

Business development is the second element of the enterprise architecture previously illustrated in Figure 5.1. Business development is defined as that group of activities, processes, and tasks that are concerned with obtaining markets and customers, while ensuring that projected revenues are sufficient to make a business case. Not coincidentally, business development is embedded in the top floor between executive leadership and product management.

Enterprise leadership sets the internal direction and policy and decides the conditions, events, operations, organizations, resource allocations, and other aspects significantly affecting and involving the enterprise. Leadership is not traditional management and control. Rather it is setting direction and then allowing the business development elements to operate within broad constraints. Leadership also provides commitment, which includes authorization, championing and sponsorship, necessary resources, and timely review and decision-making.

Enterprise vision, mission, and strategies identify the overarching business interests and objectives. These are balanced in respect to enterprise commitments already made. They become the control inputs, together with supplementary specific guidance and direction, setting the agenda for business development, which works in conjunction with other enterprise components.

The agile enterprise constantly watches and assesses itself and its environment and is quick to react to changing conditions and opportunities. This is particularly true of business development for several reasons. The first enterprise to offer a new product, or to aggressively improve an existing one, may set the standard and achieve market dominance.

Paradigm shifts open up opportunities for the agile enterprise by leveling the competitive landscape. Such shifts may occur as a result of the availability of new or improved technologies, innovations that lower price and broaden the market, changes in societal values, changes in market tastes, and other factors. For example, the Swiss invented the digital watch but spurned the concept, allowing the Japanese to produce and improve it. A seventy-plus percent market share of watch sales was reduced to single digits in less than two years, putting Swiss mechanical watchmakers out of work.

Business development is fundamentally knowledge-based. As suggested by Figure 5.6, significant effort and resources are expended collecting and assimilating information essential to the development of an in-depth understanding of both the enterprise and its environment.

Information needs with respect to the enterprise itself include knowledge of the enterprise's vision, mission, interests, direction, capabilities, core competencies, products, and technologies. Information needs with respect to the environment include knowledge of markets, customers, customer needs, competitors, competitive products, suppliers and potential partners, legal and regulatory factors, and ecological and physical environmental considerations.

This knowledge is exploited in many ways, for example, in determining:

■ What is feasible
■ What is in the enterprise's interest
■ The existence of business opportunities
■ Which opportunities to pursue
■ Technological impacts
■ Competitive position of the enterprise and its products
■ Business planning

For example, using in-depth knowledge of the enterprise's product portfolio and the market, new product developments may be targeted to fill voids in the portfolio. Knowledge of competitive products provides a basis for setting own-product requirements so as to meet, or leap ahead of, the competition. Knowledge of the technological state of the art, and

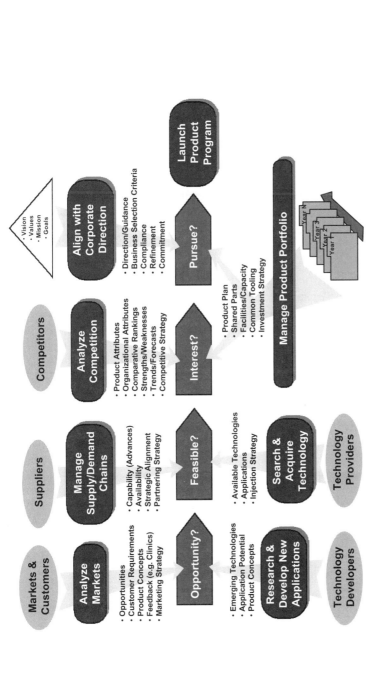

Figure 5.6 Enterprise Business Development. Information about the enterprise and its environment are critical to the decisions made during business development activities.

any deficiencies therein, may drive technology development and risk reduction investments. Make or buy and business case studies may reveal that the enterprise should team with other enterprises to form an extended enterprise rather than trying to develop or acquire a capability or technology internally.

Lean enterprises avoid pursuing too much work at one time. Business development implements this principle by using decision gates as filters. As illustrated in Figure 5.6, for any business idea, the business development activities answer four critical questions:

- Is there an opportunity
- Is it feasible to develop and manufacture the product
- Is the idea in the enterprise's interest
- Should the enterprise pursue the idea

At the first occurrence of a negative response, the idea is terminated in order to free valuable resources to develop other business opportunities.

Finding (new) business opportunities is certainly the most significant responsibility of business development; and it is a continuous cycle. But as Figure 5.7 suggests, there are important follow-on responsibilities when business opportunities result in product programs.

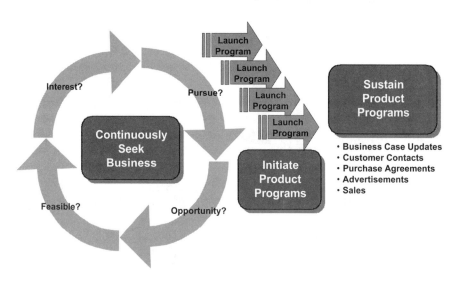

Figure 5.7 Key Business Development Activities. In addition to finding business opportunities, business development activities include launching product programs. Marketing and customer information and services are also provided during the course of a product program.

The following are among the most important considerations for pursuing a business opportunity:

- A comprehensive program plan
- An understanding of the new program's impact on existing programs and resources
- A staffing strategy
- A means of transitioning the activity from business development resources to the integrated product team that will execute the program

One of the best ways to ensure a smooth transition and program launch is to involve the IPT leaders in the final phases of the business case development and the preparation of the initial program plan. Those who must commit to the contract are also those who most rigorously challenge the assumptions and work to date. The overlap between business development and other enterprise processes are discussed further in the customer acquisition process section.

Business development resources need to be readily available to the IPT early in the product program when high-level plans are expanded and product alternatives are explored. It is the responsibility of business development to ensure that the IPT fully understands the customer needs, that the product's key features and attractiveness are not lost, and that scope creep does not exceed the parameters of the business case.

Even after a product program is successfully launched, business development continues to provide support by providing information and services with regard to the markets, customers, and business case.

Depending on how long the product development effort takes, one or more reviews of the original assumptions and estimates used in the business case are necessary. Unanticipated market shifts, competitor innovations, changes in the customer's budget priorities, and delays in the product's development can all cause a once valid business case to evaporate. Business developers, enterprise leaders, and IPT leaders must not hesitate to free up the enterprise's resources if the business case is gone and the contract becomes null and void.

Other support provided to IPTs include help with establishing and maintaining customer relations, negotiating sales and purchase agreements, and increasing customer awareness.

Ongoing marketing and advertising are used to make the enterprise and its products known and visible in the marketplace. Additional visibility enhancement derives from attendance/presentation/participation at conferences, industry forums, and special-interest meetings. Publications (e.g., articles, white papers, product brochures, and catalogs) and appearance in media and community events afford additional visibility.

Product Management

Product development and delivery activities are the mainstream of a thriving enterprise. Integrated product teams create the goods and services to satisfy customer contracts, and they support those products and the customers over the useful life of the product. Product management is the overseeing activity that coordinates and aligns the various product development activities, manages the product families as a set, and provides for collective product improvement across the product lines.

Product management, as used in this discussion, refers to all of the enterprise activities and components that contribute to developing and maintaining a variety of products (goods and services) across multiple product programs. It includes obvious activities, like internal research and development and product design during the course of a product program. However, it also includes orthogonal views of development gained by looking across multiple product lines and development efforts and by following the products into the field. Lessons learned in one product program are reviewed by all of the enterprise's other development activities for continuous improvement opportunities. Figure 5.8 illustrates the primary product management activities that surround all of the integrated product development programs.

Integrated product and process development (IPPD) is a preferred management technique emphasizing concurrent engineering of the product, the manufacturing system, and the logistic and support systems. IPPD creates an environment in which each product program addresses an entire acquisition life cycle, from the time it is a glimmer of a notion in the customer's mind until the final disposal of the product. Most product management activities and components are comprehended in IPPD, but an integrated product development program is an enterprise's response to one customer's (or class of customers') need. Product management addresses all of the customers' needs and the enterprise's ongoing capability to satisfy them. IPPD and its relationships with enterprise, product management, and product development are further discussed and illustrated under the integrated product and process development section.

The business development component is instrumental in starting any product development program, and the enterprise support components contribute to the progress of the product program. However, what makes

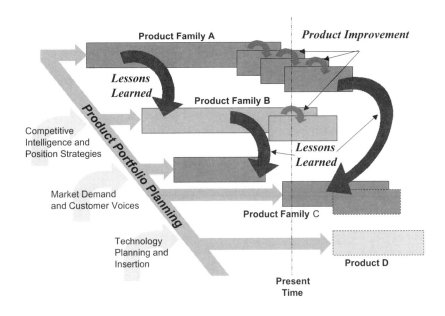

Figure 5.8 (Integrated) Product Management. Product differentiation, technology insertion, product line improvement, and application of lessons learned are the primary thrusts of product management.

a product valuable to the customer — what makes a customer choose one enterprise over another — are the core competencies executed by integrated product teams (IPT) during product development. The identification of core competencies is something that every enterprise must do for itself, but several fundamental processes must be considered, and in one form or another, probably exist in any enterprise's structure. Three core processes that every architecture should include, and every enterprise should master (in some appropriate form), as core competencies are discussed in the section on core competencies.

Departing from the traditional serial execution of the engineering and development of product first, then process (manufacturing capability), and finally logistics and support mechanisms, IPPD requires that all three major aspects of a product life cycle be considered all the time. This, of necessity, means that expertise from all disciplines must be available to the program at any time (i.e., concurrent engineering practices must be in place).

The IPT is a logical and obvious solution for the concurrency problem. An IPT is cross-functional by nature. Although the emphasis at a particular point in a product program may be on product, or manufacturing, or logistics, expert knowledge about all areas is available such that decisions are made that balance optimization of one area against potential adverse effects in the others. IPTs also include customer and supplier representation to ensure the product hits the mark, but is also realistic and feasible.

In addition, IPTs assume responsibility for schedule and budget as they develop and deliver their particular products. Effective IPTs have shown remarkable gains in quality and productivity; but creating and sustaining effective IPTs has also been shown to be a difficult and often elusive task when all of the organizational dynamics and enabling elements have not been addressed. The integrated product teams section in Chapter 2 provides additional insight into IPTs and what it takes to create the environment in which they work best.

Integrated Product and Process Development

Integrated product and process development (IPPD) is defined as "a management technique that simultaneously integrates all essential acquisition activities through use of multidisciplinary teams to optimize the design, manufacturing, business, and supportability processes" (*DoD Guide to IPPD*, 1996). IPPD is a fusion of processes with emphasis on providing the product the customer wants.

The enterprise process framework was introduced in Figure 5.3. Figure 5.9 illustrates the same framework, except that the house shape is gone and an arrow has been added to the right of each major process. This figure defines the top-level process view of the enterprise, identifying three categories of processes, which collectively comprise the enterprise: strategic, core, and support/enabling. All enterprise activities can be mapped into one of the processes listed. The arrows on the right indicate that the processes are ongoing and repeated as the enterprise performs over time.

Figure 5.10 illustrates just how much of the enterprise process framework is involved in IPPD. Notice the IPPD (customer acquisition life cycle) phases shown near the bottom of the figure. It begins with concept exploration and ends with final disposal of the product as the last event in the operation and support phase. In between are all of the activities an enterprise undertakes to define, launch, and execute a program to develop, manufacture, and deliver the desired goods and services to the customer (or class of customers).

The three-tiered area in bold outline above the IPPD life-cycle model represents a map of the various enterprise processes that play a role in

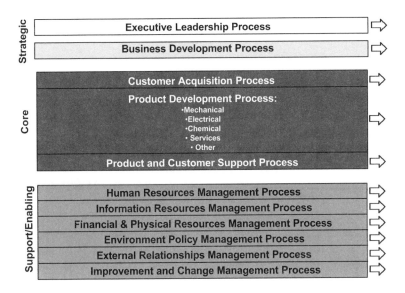

Figure 5.9 Enterprise Process Framework. This set of processes provides a foundation for understanding how cross-functional IPTs are used for integrated product development.

IPPD during each of its phases. The dominant roles each process has in an IPPD phase is suggested by a letter code. For example, in the earliest part of the concept exploration phase, the business development process is responsible (R) for developing the customer's requirements, product concepts, and a preliminary business case. It is supported (S) by resources and activities in the customer acquisition process; and all of the other functional activities consult (C) in the business development. The approval (A) for the proposed program comes from the executive leadership process.

All activities in IPPD are performed by IPTs — notice all functional areas have a role in the start-up of a product program. As the IPPD activities continue, the roles played by each functional area and process change. The IPT leadership role designated by the R moves from marketing and sales dominance, to product and manufacturing engineering, to manufacturing operations, to integrated logistics and support over the IPPD life cycle.

What is not shown in the diagram, but is a significant part of IPPD, is that the customer and the suppliers are also represented on the IPTs. As mentioned earlier, IPTs are fully collaborative teams involved in all phases and all activities (as appropriate) of the product development, delivery, and support processes.

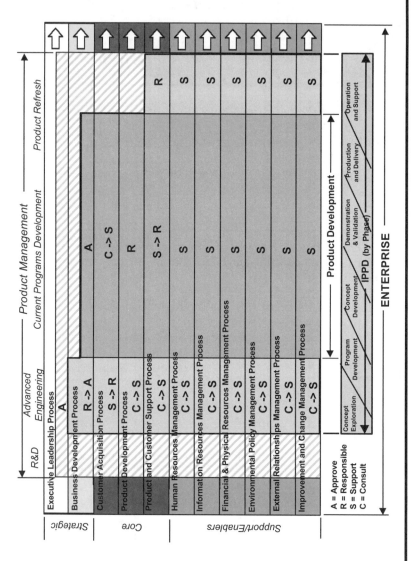

Figure 5.10 IPPD in the Process Framework. All of the enterprise processes play a role within IPPD. Cross-functional teams, supplemented by customer and supplier representatives, collaborate over the life cycle of a product acquisition.

Also outlined in Figure 5.10 is a product development process (PDP). As would be expected, PDP is the dominant process in the middle phases of IPPD. Its inclusion in the figure is a way of providing context and contrast to IPPD. A more detailed discussion of the PDP and the other two core competencies is provided in the section following this one.

Notice that IPPD is not the same as enterprise. A large amount of enterprise is given over to IPPD activities, but there are other activities an enterprise must perform in order to be ready for IPPD. If a customer were to approach an entrepreneur with a problem and an idea for a product, the entrepreneur would not want to say, "That's a great idea, I'll start an enterprise." Rather, he or she would like to say, "That's a great idea, my enterprise has been studying that new technology for some time, and we've been looking for the right moment to introduce it for one of our valued customers."

As discussed in the previous section, the product management function allows an enterprise to be ready with new product ideas and technologies in response to changes in market demand. Figure 5.10 shows the product management process surrounding (and including) the IPPD and product development processes. Notice that product management comprehends all of the enterprise activities except for strategic leadership activities performed across the enterprise by executive leadership and within the enterprise functional process bands.

As indicated by the arrows on the right side of Figure 5.10, an enterprise does not stop when a product acquisition cycle ends. Knowledge learned with one product program is transferred to other product programs. Resources made available by a program winding down are reallocated to other new or existing product programs. Thought of differently, an enterprise is an ongoing set of processes and capabilities. IPPD, by contrast, is in response to a customer's need and by definition is a finite activity. It may be a lengthy cycle; but there is a defining moment that starts the customer's search for a product, and a moment when the product is finally disposed. Product management activities and processes provide direction, scope, and continuity for many different and concurrent executions of the IPPD cycle.

As mentioned, the life cycle for a product being produced for a customer may be quite lengthy, and it may include several versions of a product by design, by a need for product enhancement, or by an opportunity for cost reduction. In this instance, portions of the linear IPPD model are iterated and the product program flow begins to cycle. Figure 5.11 illustrates the concept.

In Figure 5.11, the IPPD life cycle begins at the star when a new product is launched. It goes through a full concept development phase and enters into its initial design and manufacturing development activities.

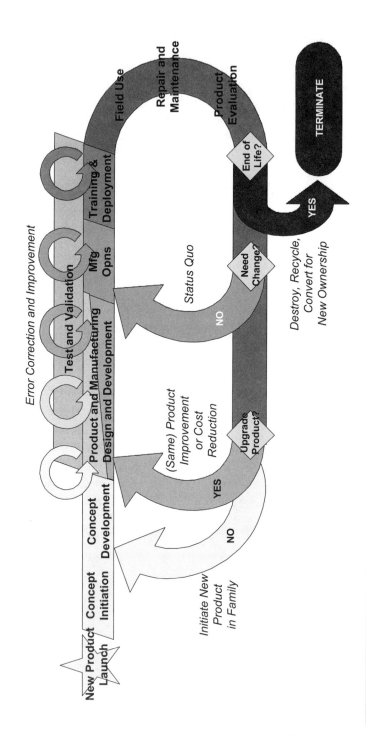

Figure 5.11 Product Program Life Cycle. As a new product goes through its initial development and deployment, and after it has been used in the field, reviews and decisions are required that result in one of four options: discontinue the product, continue as is, improve performance or reduce cost in the current product, or expand the product family. The cycle continues until all products in the family have taken the discontinue path.

Notice that both activities are concurrent but that the emphasis moves from product to manufacturing over a period of time. Testing occurs at multiple points and provides opportunities to recycle to correct errors or add improvements. As the initial product goes into manufacturing, end user training (if appropriate), deployment, field use, and repair/maintenance activities begin. At periodic intervals, or upon the occurrence of a significant event, program management (and the customer, as appropriate) make a decision about the product's future.

One option is to discontinue the product and perform any salvage, recycling, or ownership-transfer activities required to dispose of the product. Another option is simply to continue business as is — manufacturing and customer activities remain status quo. If neither of these two options is taken, then product change is implied. One option is to modify the current product, either to improve performance or to lower cost, or both. If the current product is not changed, then adding a new variant of the current product changes the product family. In either instance, appropriate phases of the IPPD life cycle are repeated in order to develop, test, produce, and deploy the revised or added product into the field or market.

Core Competencies

Core competencies are what provide value-added goods and services for customers. Three essential processes, and the resources needed to perform them, are the very foundations of an enterprise. These core processes, and how well they are executed, define the uniqueness of an enterprise that is its competitive differentiation.

The focus of this section is the core process category illustrated in Figure 5.12. Core processes are of particular significance because they make one enterprise different from the others. An enterprise needs all of the other processes to function, but from the customer's perspective, the core processes define the enterprise.

For instance, someone looking for a new automobile does not turn to Xerox, for example, because it has been identified as a world-class enterprise. It is not enlightened leadership, an attractive business prospectus, or state-of-the-art information technology that provides value for the customer who wants an automobile. Xerox's core competencies do not

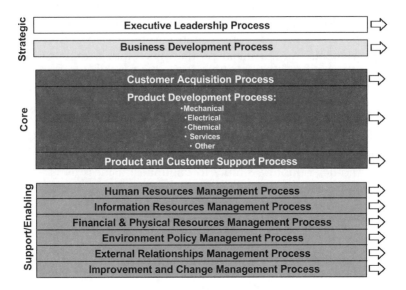

Figure 5.12   Enterprise Process Framework. The core processes of the enterprise process framework are the processes that make one enterprise different from another — they are why customers select the providers they do.

include making cars and trucks, so even though it may be a superb example of a modern enterprise, the customer's reaction is "so what?"

The customer turns to all of the enterprises with core processes that create vehicles. The automotive enterprise that executes its core processes best (that is, the most competent company) and provides the most satisfaction for the dollar (i.e., value) is the one the customer chooses. Every enterprise has core processes, but what is desired is core competency, or even better, core excellence.

Figure 5.12 identifies three core processes in the high-level enterprise architecture. The customer acquisition process fundamentally finds customers. The product development process provides the goods and service products that are demanded. And the product and customer support process sustains the products and their customers over the useful life of the products.

The customer acquisition process is an extension of the business development activity once a particular product program is launched. Its essential purpose is to find the customers for the planned product, understand their needs, negotiate their expectations of the product, and commit them to a purchase agreement. This could be something as elaborate as a competitive proposal process for winning a single-source contract to something as simple as door-to-door solicitation — but every product program needs to locate and commit (acquire) its customer(s).

The customer acquisition process includes sales, which dictates the volume and rate of production for the program. The customer acquisition process is discussed at greater length in the next section.

The product development process (PDP) is the set of activities that starts with translating customer voices into technically actionable requirements for a product and ends with the delivery of the last manufactured article. In between are all of the engineering and development activities that design and validate both the product's performance and the production systems that make it. The PDP also includes operation of the production capability that manufactures and delivers the product to its customers — starting with pilot products and low rate production, continuing with full rate production, and ending with ramp down to the last scheduled item.

Just as enterprise architecture has a taxonomy (this is discussed in Chapter 1), so does the PDP. At the highest level, an enterprise PDP is defined so that business-to-business comparisons are equitable. Stated differently, the enterprise PDP does not comprehend the products being developed, but does act as a model for all business areas and product lines to follow. General types of work, decisions, and success criteria are used to describe the enterprise PDP.

As suggested by Figure 5.12, there are several different disciplines considered within the enterprise PDP. Obviously, the high-level process for mechanical products has some differences from the one for chemical products, or electrical products, or products based on a service or information. The principal domain of expertise discipline required for each process is the difference. These processes are referred to as discipline processes.

Similar to the enterprise PDP, the discipline processes do not know the specific products being produced, but they do comprehend a class of products. The mechanical piece part process, as an example, doesn't care if the product is an engine block or a shell casing. So long as it involves metal fabrication and material removal, for example, the process is reusable. The mechanical process, however, cannot be reused if the product is a circuit card or fuel oil, which would use an electrical process or a chemical process, respectively.

For each product line, a generic PDP is tailored from the enterprise PDP and discipline processes. For example, a diversified aerospace company such as Raytheon may have a generic PDP for each of its radar, missile, microelectronics, and aircraft product lines. A generic PDP comprehends the product family, its technologies, and the customers who need them. A generic PDP provides metrics that allow fair comparisons among technically similar programs. For example, the radar PDP is the benchmark by which to compare a program providing a ground-based sensor for the Army to one providing the same basic technologies in a marine radar for small commercial boats.

At the business unit level, programs are compared via the generic PDP criteria. At the detailed work level, however, each program has a specific development process that understands the particulars of the product and the product's customer. The previously mentioned program for the Army has unique requirements placed on it, and in such a case, the generic radar PDP is tailored into a specific program PDP. The PDP is discussed further later in this chapter.

The product and customer support process starts with the requirements, design, and validation of the complementary products and services needed to maintain, repair, modify, and enhance the products after delivery. The process also provides all of the goods and services needed to educate, train, and accommodate the customers in the operation of the product throughout its useful life. Similarly, any special material and tools to service the product are made available to the customers and others intended to maintain the product. The support process ends only with the final disposal of the last functional article. Additional insight into the product and customer support process is provided in the product and customer support process section

Customer Acquisition Process

The business development component identifies the initial target markets and customers, but it is up to the individual product programs to follow through with the details. IPT interactions with the customers during the course of development and delivery are critical for keeping a program on target; and the actual purchase agreements negotiated before and during a program provide its business controls. Business development resources participate in and provide ongoing support for the IPT as it executes the customer acquisition process.

No product program gets launched without having had a preliminary business case proposed to and approved by enterprise leadership. This preliminary case is prepared by the business development component as part of its process (refer to the section on business development). However, after a product program is initiated, the initial business case is maintained and updated by marketing and sales activities executed during the course of product development and delivery. This is one of the key responsibilities of the customer acquisition process.

Best commercial practices involve market clinics and focus groups to gather early customer reactions to the prototypal product. Pre-production mock-ups, early development concepts, and product prototypes are shared with representative cross sections of the intended market to confirm that the product's performance and price still represent good value to the intended customers. The customer acquisition process includes such clinics and focus groups to help ensure the product stays on target for maximum customer satisfaction.

Developing product awareness and a competitive position within the market is also a key activity in the customer acquisition process. Where products are developed to supply a class of customers and their generic needs (automobiles, appliances, clothing, for example), tradeshows, advertisements, and product demonstrations are techniques used to make potential customers aware of both future and current products. As part of making customers aware of a product, it is important to create an understanding of what is unique, special, or different about the product. To create an edge, the customer acquisition process must make it easy for the customers to understand how its product is superior to the competition and why purchasing the product represents a worthwhile and satisfying experience.

Even if a product development program is for a single customer, that customer must be aware of the product during all phases of activity. Just as the architect starts with conceptual drawings to make the homebuyer aware of what the house will look like, the customer acquisition process provides the customer with early and frequent exposure to the intended product. Drawings, mock-ups, display rapid-prototyping, and simulations (including virtual reality demonstrations) are all best-practice techniques used to project the eventual product and its usage to the customer during the earliest phases of development. Customer awareness and feedback are especially significant during the analysis and validation of product requirements. A world-class implementation of a product for which the customer has no use should be every businessperson's nightmare.

As a product moves into its detailed engineering phase, there are typically numerous suggestions for improvements made by the product and manufacturing engineers. It is important that the customer's perspective be considered when evaluating any suggested improvement. If better performance, higher quality, increased reliability or durability, decreased maintenance, lower cost, or earlier delivery is apparent, then the suggestion is in the customer's value stream and is usually readily accepted. If, however, the improvement is not apparent to the customer, then caution must be taken. If the improvement is transparent to the customer (that is, if no penalty is perceived), the improvement may be implemented.

If, however, a suggested improvement offers an advantage in one aspect of the product but requires some sacrifice in another aspect, the customer must be involved in the decision. The same is true when unforeseen difficulties prevent the design from achieving its original goals within the allocated budget and schedule. Honest communication gives the customer the information needed to understand the problem and the options. The customer's priorities and preferences must be established. Any subsequent changes in the performance, scope, cost, or delivery schedule of the product must honor those priorities in order to sustain customer confidence and satisfaction in the purchase experience.

The customer acquisition process includes contract administration, change negotiation, and additional sales as an extension of the business development process — especially in instances where the contract includes the product development activities themselves. Where product development and initial manufacturing are performed in anticipation of market needs and responses, sales and delivery activities are included in the customer acquisition process. At a minimum this must address providing initial product inventories, sales tracking, and inventory replenishment.

The customer acquisition process must ensure accurate delivery timing. Product delivery before the need date does little to foster customer satisfaction. Even worse is a missed delivery date because the seller promised something that was not realistically possible. Manufacturing capability and capacity are traded against negotiated delivery dates — demand drives production rates; capacity constrains delivery dates.

Agile and flexible manufacturing strategies and facilities are key enablers for responding to fluctuations in market pull. Configurable cells that can be quickly changed from production of a product or product model that is not selling as well as projected to production of a hot product are vital. Not only must the manufacturing tooling change, but the people who operate the equipment must be versatile. Similarly, the logistic methods and systems that deliver raw material and take away finished goods must also be agile and easily adaptable.

Product Development Process

The product development process (PDP) is what creates and delivers the actual goods and services to the customers. In the past, product creation has been thought of as an internal, inventive activity, but IPPD calls for the PDP to be a supportive, synthesis process that is always fully aware of how the product is going to be used and how it is going to be built and serviced.

This section only highlights some of the key aspects of the PDP. Abundant material in other documents provides additional details.

■ The PDP starts with the first translation of customer requirements into a set of technical requirements for a product or service. Customer and marketing representation on the IPT is the best way to ensure that the original intent of the customer voices are preserved in the technical parameters used by engineering. The PDP ends when the last article scheduled for production has been delivered to its customer.

■ The PDP is the dominant set of activities and resources required by IPPD — especially for manufacturing enterprises. The ability to design and manufacture products well is the very foundation of enterprise. Good intentions for meeting the customer's needs and elegant apologies made while fixing a product are poor second choices for the customer who is about to select one manufacturer's product over another's.

■ The ability to execute this core competency quickly and accurately is the primary competitive edge for being first to market and best in class. Robust design strategies, component sharing and reuse, adoption of standards, computer-aided engineering, design, and manufacturing (CAE, CAD, and CAM, respectively), and common processes are key enablers for shortened product development times. Systems engineering, six sigma, Taguchi methods, and integrated validation techniques built into the development processes are the key enablers for first-time quality.

■ It must be recognized that the product, the capabilities to manufacture it, and the capabilities to support it are considered all at once during the PDP. Concurrent engineering is an imperative for best-practice integrated product development. All of the best practices mentioned above apply equally to the product, the manufacturing systems, and the support systems.

■ The PDP understands the long shadow concept — 80 to 90 percent of a product's manufacturing and maintenance costs are engineered into the product during early concept analysis and selection. Total ownership cost and cost as an independent variable (CAIV) are significant concepts to be factored into the PDP processes and design selection criteria.

■ Product and manufacturing designs need to trade single product and manufacturing facility optimization against the idea of component sharing and reusability within and across the enterprise's diversified product lines. If it were up to any one customer, the entire enterprise would be dedicated to his or her product. The enterprise must look across multiple product development efforts and decide what provides the most satisfaction for the highest number of customers. Agile enterprise needs must be traded against lean manufacturing optimizations made for one customer or class of customers.

■ Virtual collocation, integrated and globally accessible information, and advanced simulation and modeling techniques are key enablers for the PDP, especially when a complex product is being developed by a coalition acting as an extended enterprise. The use of modern information technology is a given for these capabilities — refer to the section on information resources managment for additional insight into how managing information resources is fundamental to enterprise today.

Leverage of Models, Simulation, and Lessons Learned for PDP

The knowledge that results from integrating lessons learned with the increasing sophistication of math-based computer models allows robust product designs.

Many enterprises today make their business lessons learned (corporate knowledge) readily available to others. Books, briefings, seminars, and Web sites offer insight into what has gone well and not gone well, and they suggest improvements that teams and companies have gained through experience. The widespread availability of such corporate knowledge provides the opportunity to quickly and easily obtain information to help reduce the possibility and probability of repeating mistakes or being continually learning the hard way. A knowledge management process of supporting tools for capturing, accessing, and applying lessons learned is clearly a best practice for any enterprise.

Mistakes during product design and development are inevitable. The variations are in their number, significance, and overall impact. Because of the time and the money required to produce prototype hardware and design the associated production processes, the cost of rework for errors detected late in the PDP can be extremely high. By contrast, design errors found early in the PDP (i.e., during the paper product phase) are relatively quick and inexpensive to fix.

By using math-based computer modeling and simulation routines, product, manufacturing, and service design alternatives can be evaluated, choices can be made, and designs can be confirmed prior to the first piece of hardware being manufactured. Virtual reality techniques and tools, as an example, allow developers to interactively examine three-dimensional representations of the product and it usage and the factory and its operation.

Improvements in the sophistication and maturity of simulation and analysis tools will continue the trends in reduced product and process development times and overall program costs through:

- Increased use of what-if scenarios to provide rigorous design analysis and evaluation, design alternative trade studies, and heightened confidence in the chosen solution
- Automated design optimization
- Reduced reliance on the use of prototype hardware
- Reduced downstream change activity, false starts, and surprises

When lessons learned are integrated into modeling and simulation algorithms and this combination is refined and bounded with engineering design rules, the resulting capability can yield very robust, and first-time capable, product and process design.

Product and Customer Support Process

The cost and quality of service after delivery are significant determinants in whether a customer chooses to do business with an enterprise again. Establishing long-term relationships with valued customers forms a stable base for enterprise longevity and growth.

Except for commodities, where product price and quality are essentially the only purchase considerations, most customers are significantly influenced by the post-delivery experience. The availability of the item or service, and the ease and cost of product maintenance or enhancement, have considerable influence on repeat business.

Customers form their opinions of an enterprise through what they experience; and for the most part, they experience the sales, delivery, and service processes. The excellence of those processes and the people who execute them are essential for customer satisfaction. In those instances where the customer participates directly in product development as a member of an IPT, the quality of all the other processes required for IPPD also contribute to the customer's impression of an enterprise.

Satisfied customers are valuable assets in two ways: they buy again and they recommend the enterprise to others. The exact opposite is true of dissatisfied customer — not only do they not spend their own money again, their expression of a bad experience acts as a deterrent to other potential customers.

Clearly, the importance of this phase of IPPD suggests that positive post-delivery experiences must be a key part of the product development strategies. Integrated logistics planning must be comprehended in the product design and spares production.

Best-practice enablers for rewarding customer support experiences include the following:

- Easy access to and visualization of product data
- Easy ordering mechanisms
- Prompt and accurate order fulfillment
- Easy access to cost-effective maintenance
- An easy-to-use grievance procedure, with prompt and fair responses
- Proactive follow-up and solicitation of ideas for product and service improvement (these help in continuous improvement)
- Incentives and rewards for repeat business and referrals (these provide customers with a sense of ownership and participation in the enterprise)

Enterprise Support/Enabling

Sustaining and enabling capabilities are needed in every enterprise. However, support activities and resources must be as lean as possible since they are, by definition, not in the customer's value stream. Providing more capability than is needed may hurt the enterprise's competitiveness.

Every enterprise needs sustaining and enabling capabilities to support it. These capabilities, however, must be analyzed in light of other enterprise capabilities and processes, especially the core competencies. Optimization or enhancement of support processes based solely on an internal perspective may introduce inefficiencies in the core capabilities and processes, resulting in diminished enterprise performance and lower product quality.

An example would be an enterprise implementing a just-in-time (JIT) strategy in its core manufacturing processes. When analyzing what components are affected by this strategy, it would seem clear that supply chain management, procurement, and receiving and material handling components are significant in the supply side. Knowledge of suppliers' capabilities and delivery methods is needed to avoid maintaining a large stock of raw materials.

On the demand side, close contact with the customers must also be maintained, usually via sales data, to ensure delivery of the correct volume of end product. Not enough volume means lost sales; too much volume means loss of profit caused by increasing storage costs, sales incentives, and liquidation. It is also clear that the information management technology and processes provided by the information resources component (refer to the information resources managment section) will be key in the JIT implementation.

The question here is, How good does the information management system have to be? Depending on the business, this may not be as critical as it would appear on the surface. If there are a limited number of suppliers and only a few different customers, a best-in-class or state-of-the-art information system may not be required. To stay competitive may only require examining and modifying the current processes. The cost of upgrading or installing a new information system may not be justified. Reevaluation of the JIT strategy may also be in order as part of the information management support analysis.

The sections that follow identify the most significant enterprise support and enabling capabilities. Not every facet of these capabilities is explored; however, those aspects or features that are of special significance to totally integrated enterprise are highlighted.

Human Resources Management

How personnel are selected, deployed, utilized, and rewarded in an integrated enterprise using IPTs differs from the HR practices of traditional enterprises.

Human resources management plays a significant role for integrated enterprises. Personnel selection, deployment, performance, and rewards are based on an IPT environment. This is a collaborative environment. A virtual, extended enterprise requires collaboration and teamwork both inside and outside the core enterprise. Providing the personnel who can work in teams with different corporations and suppliers in a virtual, collaborative IPPD environment is the primary challenge for human resource management.

Human resources (HR) encompasses such elements as

- Determining job skills (level and mix) needed by the enterprise
- Recruiting and retaining personnel with the necessary skills
- Personnel management (resource allocation)
- Employee development (personal, professional, and career)
- Employee performance measurement and feedback
- Employee compensation, rewards, and recognition
- Employee well-being, satisfaction, and involvement in the enterprise
- Labor/management relations
- HR information

The IPT-oriented enterprise selects employees based on a set of needs different from those in traditional enterprises. Emphasis is placed not only on technical competency, but interpersonal skills as well. Skill sets required by enterprise processes optimize the IPT rather than any one discipline, individual, project, or program.

In some cases, personnel are hired for functions having no exact analog in the traditional standalone enterprise. For example, a lean and agile prime contractor, recognizing that it can succeed only in an environment in which its suppliers are also lean and agile, hires lean/agile experts to deploy among the suppliers. The job of these experts is to inculcate the lean/agile philosophy while assisting the suppliers in transforming themselves into lean and agile enterprises.

Another area of divergence between lean/agile and traditional enterprises is in regard to compensation, rewards, and recognition. Compensation, rewards, and recognition are performance-based in the lean/agile enterprise. Significantly, a substantial portion of these items is bound to IPT performance, rather than just individual performance. One-time bonuses (or lack thereof) tied to the IPT's ability to meet or exceed its cost, schedule, and quality commitments replace the notions of annual cost-of-living and seniority raises. Increases in base salary are tied to demonstrable gains in an employee's capabilities, not the number of years served at a particular grade. More of an employee's annual compensation is at risk; i.e., tied to the performance of the IPT and the enterprise (in the form of profit sharing).

Still another difference exists in the manner of personnel deployment. Unlike the traditional approach in which people are simply assigned to any project where needed, membership in IPTs is contingent on the approval of other team members. A 360-degree review allows team members to provide feedback on peer performance. Team members are empowered and encouraged to help each other learn and excel at the needed skills and activities. However, a member who, in the IPT's judgment, fails to attain a sufficient level of excellence and performance may ultimately be expelled from the IPT. This power of the IPT to hire and fire its members is a necessary consequence of the fact that the IPT is compensated, rewarded, and recognized based on its success and performance.

Roles and job descriptions also differ between traditional and lean/agile enterprises. Management roles, per se, are redefined to be primarily concerned with removing obstacles that impair IPT performance and ensuring sufficient support and resources. Management is, therefore, an enabling and facilitating job rather than a command and control job.

IPTs persist only for the span of time they are needed. At the conclusion of an IPT's purpose, its members are released back to their home organizations or are redeployed in other IPTs. This suggests still another difference between traditional and IPT-oriented enterprises.

The traditional functional organizations are transformed into personnel enabling centers and assume many of the HR roles — especially those concerned with job satisfaction, employee development, and career planning. The functional homeroom has an enterprise-wide perspective and is vitally involved in planning the resources needed for the enterprise's projected operations. As such, the homeroom, not the IPT, is in the best position to advise employees about the training and development they need to be best positioned for a rewarding career within the enterprise.

Information Resources Management

Information resources management provides for information planning; data-, information-, and knowledge-management processes; and technology needed by the enterprise to sustain its operations and make informed decisions.

Information is a strategic resource for the enterprise. Successful information management and implementation begins with effective planning. A view of data and information from the enterprise perspective is needed to effectively manage this valuable enterprise asset. Data management strategies and implementation plans are derived from the requirements of the enterprise. Data elements must be organized before they can be accessed and integrated into exploitable information. The organization of data and the use of metadata (data about the data) elements are key considerations in understanding the requirements for selecting and implementing an enabling technology to exploit information.

The information technology (IT) view of the enterprise describes the technology enablers for operating the enterprise. The IT view may be referred to as an enterprise-wide information technology infrastructure view, or just information technology infrastructure view (ITIV) for short. The ITIV is the enabling infrastructure for the evolution of the enterprise information architectures. The primary objective of the ITIV is to achieve interoperability within the enterprise. The architecture will define a logical structure able to give any enterprise activity appropriate access to required information.

Figure 5.13 illustrates processes, data (data types), and technology within the enterprise. They all interact with each other within the ITIV.

Collaboration, partnerships, and mergers create multicompany enterprises. Portals, vortals, BI portals, and B2B technology continue to create solutions based on a specific software package-to-package paradigm.

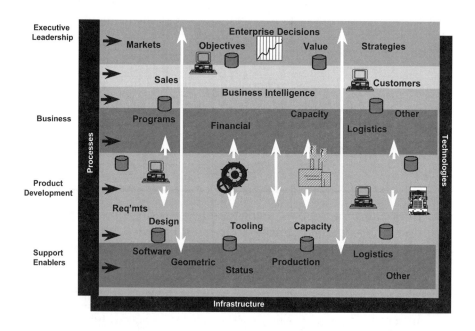

Figure 5.13 Information Resources Management. Various types of information, defined and organized by processes, supported by infrastructure, and injected with technology, are managed to sustain the enterprise and facilitate informed decisions.

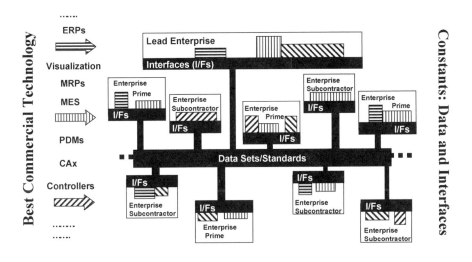

Figure 5.14   Multi-Company Virtual Enterprise. This option establishes protocols of knowledge consisting of interface and data definitions/standards that represent the core architecture enablers for the integration of enterprises.

The normal attitude is to address specific areas and functional needs of the enterprise one at a time. Figure 5.14 illustrates the multicompany virtual enterprise (MCVE). This is an option that establishes protocols of knowledge consisting of interface and data definitions/standards that represent the core architecture enablers for the integration of enterprises.

If we look at enterprise application integration (EAI), for example, we see that there are two fundamental levels of integration: data and business. Integrating at the business level is often desirable within a particular business entity, but is generally impractical as we extend the enterprise to embrace partners in a collaborative endeavor. To integrate at the business level is to deal with specific application, business rules and processes, and user interfaces. This is difficult enough within one's own organization, and virtually impossible across enterprises. Data standards, on the other hand, can exist outside the application and therefore stand alone. It is the simplest form of integration.

The first step in enabling and creating the MCVE is to define the interface specification by which everyone will operate. Where possible, select (public) open standards, and avoid proprietary systems no matter how attractive they may appear in the short term. Internet standards will define the mechanism for data transport among members of the virtual enterprise.

Interface layers will have to be designed so that various enterprise components can plug in at will. Industry standards are evolving to facilitate seamless data exchanges, regardless of the source application.

Financial and Physical Resource Management

Financial and physical resources are proactively managed to maximize benefits to the enterprise. This involves a degree of fiscal candor not typically associated with traditional enterprises.

Financial and physical resources must be managed with consideration for all the other components within the enterprise. This section highlights some facets of traditional financial and physical resource management that may differ in a virtual, agile, and lean enterprise.

The fundamental change in traditional financial management strategies made by best-practice enterprises seems to be a matter of who is made aware of, and responsible for, financial data and performance. In traditional enterprise, the accounting ledgers were closely held by a privileged few. The everyday worker was told to worry about doing his or her job and that someone else would worry about the money.

Modern enterprises, especially those using integrated product teams, make everyone in the enterprise aware of the financial realities of the business. IPTs are held accountable for budget performance as well as for schedule and product performance. The customer and supplier representatives on the IPTs also have access to the budgetary data. This openness with numbers requires substantial change in traditional organizational culture. It also requires solid corporate citizenship and the utmost in ethical behavior by everyone in and associated with the enterprise.

The advantage of making everyone aware of cost is that employees understand better how to help eliminate waste and improve cost-effectiveness. If profit-sharing bonuses for all employees are at stake, there seems to be no limit to the number of suggestions provided by employees once they understand the financial parameters of the business as well as the technical and performance requirements.

The enterprise's funds must be budgeted, allocated, and managed in accordance with defined plans and priorities, rather than simply being handed out as demand arises. Control of funds is used at all levels of the enterprise as a primary means of ensuring that the right things are being done by the right people at the right time. Expenditure tracking is performed over time as the expenditures occur, rather than being reconstructed after the fact in an attempt to determine where the money went after it is too late to exert control. Attention is constantly given to ensuring that the value derived is commensurate with the money expended and to guarantee that the work remains strongly correlated with the plans and priorities.

Another financial best practice is the idea of management reserve. As part of program risk management and mitigation, a reserve of uncommitted funds is budgeted. In the event unplanned contingencies arise, reserve funds are allocated on a case-by-case basis. Increased funds are not always the answer to a program's problems — scope and performance changes, schedule modification, and deferred delivery are also program alternatives. But if there is no planned reserve, then it's not even an option.

If contingency costs exceed the available reserve and other options are not in the enterprise's best interest, another financial best practice comes into play — the prioritized portfolio. One or more low-priority projects or programs are deferred or cancelled outright, and their funds are redirected to backfill the contingency. This requires financial planners to be vitally involved in portfolio development. Those programs critical to the enterprise's viability must be clearly differentiated from those that are additional opportunities when the circumstances allow.

Across-the-board marginal funding cuts in competing project and program allocations are not used to meet contingency requirements. This traditional lawn mower approach to budget reduction has two dangerous effects. First, lean programs are unduly penalized, perhaps to the point where they can no longer succeed. If this happens to vital programs, the enterprise has done unspeakable damage to itself. Second, a history of blanket cuts invites every program and organization to build in fat as protection against the inevitable next pass of the financial lawnmower. The vicious cycle of padding for cuts and cutting for pads makes the idea of accurate financial planning and accounting all but impossible.

Physical resources must also be proactively managed to maximize benefits to the enterprise. Facilities planners must be totally involved in portfolio development. Laying plans for product programs that have no available facilities or equipment for development and manufacture is pointless. Capital investments in new or modernized buildings and equipment are an integral part of portfolio development and planning.

Another aspect of portfolio planning involves resource leveling, including facilities and equipment. For example, an enterprise having a number of product programs all requiring use of the same production facility and equipment may have to phase, or stagger, the programs in time in order to level the demand curve, despite the desires of each program's management. This may entail such actions as rationing scarce assets to the detriment of any given project or program. Conversely, only by managing scarce resources in an integrated manner at the enterprise level can we ensure that commitments are not made to customers that result in schedule conflicts or exceeding the available capacity.

Notice that organizational culture again comes into play. Each program must know its place in the overall sequence, and each must relinquish the scarce resource when it is time. Everyone must understand what is best for the enterprise and be rewarded for cooperation. Trust in and respect for the other programs and the enterprise decision-makers are required.

The design of physical resources is also impacted by other enterprise best practices. Lean manufacturing techniques place expectations on the physical configuration of manufacturing plants. Large receiving and shipping storage areas are no longer useful. Material handling in small lots becomes important — the idea is to move a raw material or component lot directly from its shipping device (e.g., a truck or rail car) to its processing or assembly station. This implies many external access points and short paths to the processing stations.

Long lines dedicated to a specific product manufacture are replaced by flexible manufacturing cells, typically configured in a U-shaped pattern. Large, stationary tools, each dedicated to a single product process, are replaced by movable, configurable, multipurpose tools with computer-based intelligence. As a result of the need to rearrange floor space easily and rapidly, the plant's infrastructure must be able to deliver electronic information, water, and electrical, hydraulic, and pneumatic power to virtually any point on an otherwise unfettered work floor. For example, a standard, high-quality, broad-bandwidth electronic information port should be no more than 20 feet away from any point in the facility.

Visual and audible control mechanisms are also integral parts of a lean manufacturing plant. Acoustic management and line-of-sight considerations become more significant factors in physical plant design.

Office area design is also impacted by some of the best practices for using integrated product teams and computer-aided enterprise processes. Open office space (for example, low-wall cubicle clusters) accelerates collaborative team performance. In turn, this requires employees to learn modified office etiquette, particularly in regard to voice levels used for phone calls and conversations. The need for frequent team interaction creates an increased demand for conference areas. The ratio of conference area to office area is substantially different for the collaborative enterprise, compared to the traditional office. As teams are created, modified, and disbanded, office areas are altered. Modular office equipment and robust infrastructure are enablers for an agile office environment.

Because so much of the information created in the office environment is now computer-based, the office information technology infrastructure (as discussed in the previous section) is a significant consideration for facility design. Access to enterprise information and the ability to project it in conference areas become key enablers. They save the time and cost of creating presentations in other media and allow ready access to facts and data as questions are posed during the course of a conference. Decision-making is greatly facilitated.

The ability to electronically record, review, and post minutes and action items (or even the meeting itself) as a routine matter during a conference saves time and errors in sharing the results of a conference with others. Videoconferencing capability among different extended enterprise locations saves travel time and costs.

Environmental Policy Management

Heightened societal sensitivity to environmental issues, evidenced by laws and frequent media attention, has elevated environmental considerations from an incidental issue to a primary concern across the enterprise.

Three-Mile Island. Bhopal. Chernobyl. Exxon Valdez. These names are engraved in the minds of billions as manmade disasters both ecological and human. Consequences have included thousands of dead and injured, relocation of populations, clean-up costs in the billions of dollars, endless legal combat, negative publicity and societal relations, and the passage of conservative laws. Each was the responsibility of one or more enterprises. Each is now the burden of those same enterprises (assuming that they even still exist).

The potential adverse impact an enterprise may have on the environment and, as a consequence, on its own well being is self-evident. This is one reason it is imperative that enterprises establish policy and environmental management programs that proactively address environmental issues.

A second reason for proactive environmental policy management is to participate in industry special-interest groups as a means of influencing laws and regulations. An example where having a responsible environmental position from which to influence legislators is provided by the experience of the chemical industry.

In the mid- to late-1990s, the chemical industry became aware of a political initiative to impose broad restrictions on the use of chlorine-containing chemicals. The perceived need for change arose out of concern about environmental releases of a relatively select group of hazardous chlorine-containing compounds. The chemical industry has successfully argued that the use of alternatives to chlorine-containing bleaches, salt, medicines, and other beneficial chlorinated compounds — if such even existed at all — were, in some cases, worse than the original compounds that authorities threatened to ban or restrict. Moreover, the beneficial use of chlorinated compounds is so huge that to ban or restrict them is an extreme action that would cause large-scale economic disruptions.

In addition to ethical and self-interest considerations, legal requirements provide additional incentive for enterprises to establish environmental policy and proactive management programs. These programs provide a formal, unifying mechanism for satisfying legal obligations for dealing with hazardous material (HAZMAT), to include such things as workplace and community safety plans and procedures, warnings and notifications, handling, disposal, and incident remediation and reporting.

Best-practice enterprises exceed the minimum (mandated) requirement by embracing a systems-level view of environmental issues (see Figure 5.15). At a fairly basic level, recycling of materials (both manufactured waste and the recovered product) is practiced. At a somewhat higher level, recycled materials are translated into a revenue-generating marketable commodity. At the highest level, systematic, end-to-end consideration is given to all processes and chemicals used, their life-cycle costs, and their life-cycle impacts (including, e.g., disposal, reusability, etc.). Then conscious decisions are made to select low-environmental-impact processes that use relatively benign chemicals.

This systemic view of environmental impact includes all aspects of the product life cycle. The development and manufacturing processes and byproducts, the operation of the product and byproducts, the maintenance processes and byproducts, and the disposal/recycling processes and byproducts are all considered in the environmental strategies.

External Relationships Management

Increased communication and transportation capabilities have made virtually every market sector a global arena with more competitors than ever. Enterprises are becoming increasingly interdependent, as traditionally vertical companies divest noncore capabilities and outsource for more services. As a result, managing relationships with elements external to the enterprise becomes more important than ever.

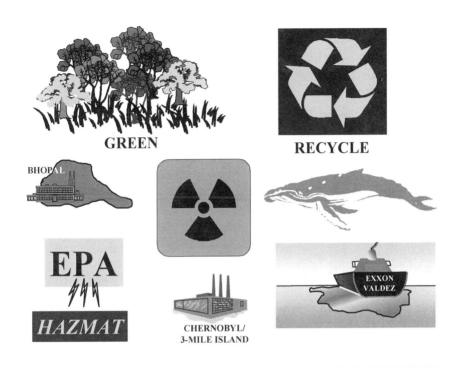

GREEN

RECYCLE

BHOPAL

EPA

HAZMAT

CHERNOBYL/
3-MILE ISLAND

EXXON
VALDEZ

Figure 5.15 Environmental Policy Management Issues. The best practice enterprise implements a formal policy and environmental management program as a matter of self-interest and ethical environmental stewardship.

An enterprise's external relationships are wide-ranging. As suggested by Figure 5.16, four broad categories of external relationships demand an enterprise's attention: business relationships, government relationships, financial relationships, and relationships with the public at large. Whether relationships are mutually supportive or adversarial has an immense impact on the enterprise's ability to survive and prosper.

Every enterprise is well aware of government relationships, if for no other reason than tax regulations. Also, there is an increasing number of directives involving safety and worker rights. The point for extended enterprise is simply that as more interdependencies are established across state and national boundaries, the complexity of understanding and complying with the increased number of government rules and regulations grows accordingly. Best-practice enterprises have government watch-groups that monitor pending legislation and legal proceedings and alert the enterprises to possible changes. This allows the enterprises to prepare contingency plans for proactive change.

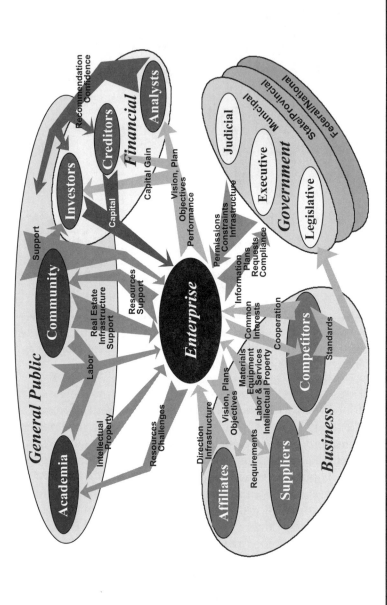

Figure 5.16 External Relationships Management. Enterprise is highly dependent on successful relationships with many outside elements. Management that creates win–win relationships puts the enterprise in the best position to prosper.

Any business that is publicly owned must be acutely aware of the influence of the stock market. As the number of people that use the Internet to actively trade stock increases, the more important it becomes to provide adequate information about the enterprise and its status to avoid rapid fluctuations in market valuation. Analysts become very important to the potential investor's perception of an enterprise. Recommendations that the analysts make or withhold are widely accessible. The number of traders who can act on the advice makes each nuance or inflection in an analysis a possible trigger for a buying or selling spree. Informed investors tend to make more predictable decisions. Best-practice enterprises communicate often and honestly with their investors, their creditors, and those who assess the financial potential of the business.

Best-practice enterprises recognize that finding and retaining qualified employees are important tasks. Good relationships with the general public can make the human resources recruiting task much easier. Two specific areas in the public domain warrant proactive relationship development.

Enterprises that need well-trained employees help themselves when they actively support educational institutions. Equipment that is no longer needed, grants, scholarships, and personnel willing to serve as mentors and coaches are provided to academic institutions. In exchange, the enterprise gets a voice about what students need to learn to be better prepared to enter the labor force. Enterprises also benefit from close relationships with academia by being better positioned to gain insight into research. Finally, a positive presence on campus translates into a competitive advantage in recruiting.

Best-practice enterprises also invest in their local communities. The enterprise that makes the area a better place to live gains the loyalty of employees because their total quality of life is improved. Public admiration translates into a ready source of labor that is already in the area (minimal relocation costs) and needn't go through any period of cultural adjustment (lower employee turnover). Community members become civic partners ready to work with an enterprise when changes require real estate transactions, permits and licenses, abatements, incentives, and infrastructure changes, as examples.

For the enterprise that sells to the public at large, advertising and public awareness programs that establish good corporate citizenship are also good investments. All other issues being equal, consumers tend to favor the companies they admire most when making purchasing decisions. Another potential benefit of public esteem is that potential employees seek out the enterprise; such applicants tend to be highly motivated to succeed when they get work with their company of choice.

Business relationships, of course, are the mainstay of extended enterprise. As enterprises focus more on core competencies and turn to allies for supplemental services and goods, it becomes increasingly significant to communicate with other enterprises and seek mutually supportive strategies. This includes dialogue with direct competitors about issues and topics that are shared concerns about the business environment or emergent technology, not the products that are the basis of competition.

For example, major American automotive manufacturers joined a consortium, with suppliers and academia, to study and develop advanced electric battery technology. The cost of major research and development was realistically beyond the capability of any one of them, but collectively they could afford to seek an enabling technology. The automotive manufacturers do not benefit directly (i.e., they do not make batteries), but advances in the technology allow the enterprises to improve their automotive products (each in its own undisclosed way) as they compete for new vehicle sales.

Another best practice for competitive enterprises involves the development and support of industry standards. This doesn't necessarily involve international committees taking years to develop *de jure* standards, although that is not to be ignored. It more likely involves frank discussions about creating *de facto* standards for infrastructure and nondifferentiators (i.e., internal functions and components that are not visible to the customer and therefore do not influence the purchase decision).

Clearly, proprietary technology has been one of the principal competitive advantages in enterprises that manufacture goods; and no one expects that to change. However, there is a fine line between having a better mousetrap and creating a bottleneck to progress. If a proprietary technology creates a perceived monopoly, there are often legal repercussions as evidenced by several governmental oversight committees. Microsoft's protracted involvement in a federal inquiry is a prime example. Even if the technology is determined not to be a monopoly, if it creates a perceived all or nothing choice for purchasers, the seeds of destruction are planted.

It may seem desirable to dictate to the market while the technology is current, but it places the enterprise in a completely defensive posture. While other enterprises are forced to push for better technology, the proprietary enterprise must defend its markets with aging technology. What was once a clear advantage becomes a distinct liability once new technology enters the market. Even if an enterprise replaces its own technology, it must be careful of market backlash. Customers who feel they were forced one direction, only to have a better alternative surface almost immediately, tend to think in terms of planned obsolescence or a bait-and-switch ploy. Neither perception is likely to result in repeat or increased sales.

Cooperation that adds to interoperability and easy deployment into the market makes a great deal of sense. The old, but still appropriate, analogy is about getting a bigger piece of pie. One paradigm is a fight in which one competitor must take from the other — it's a zero-sum game that has a winner but demands a loser. The best-practice paradigm creates a larger pie, and everyone gets a bigger piece. When competitors work together to create attractive and affordable value for customers, the number of buyers increases such that each enterprise can prosper.

For the agile, lean enterprise one set of relationships that may differ considerably from the traditional is that of supplier relationships. Nowhere is this more evident than in the manner in which enterprises identify, engage, manage, and cooperate with key suppliers.

The best practice enterprise adopts a philosophy that the suppliers' success is the enterprise's success. To ensure this success, the enterprise takes such specific actions as incorporating the supplier into its IPPD process, seeking proactive supplier involvement early in programs when important decisions are being made, collocating enterprise personnel with supplier personnel to effect open and timely communications, and other measures.

Supplier selection traditionally hinges on such criteria as price, quality, scale, schedule, and responsiveness. Agile and lean enterprises also attach great importance to additional considerations having a direct impact on competitiveness. One method of avoiding high costs is not to develop or duplicate things in-house that may be acquired more effectively externally. This strategy may be enabled by judiciously choosing suppliers already possessing the requisite complementary technologies, capabilities, and products.

In some industries the high cost of new product development has become prohibitive with respect to the feasibility of any single enterprise undertaking such efforts. This has resulted in instances of consortia that collectively assume the cost, risk, and rewards. An alternative approach is for one or more system integrators (sometimes referred to as prime contractors) to subcontract significant portions of the development and its associated cost, risk, and reward to suppliers. In the best-practice enterprise, these major subcontractors are considered so important to the success of the program that they are brought into the IPPD activities and participate in the IPTs.

Alliances and partnerships result in extended enterprises possessing, in aggregate, the requisite capabilities that none of them singly possesses. Collaborative processes and technologies must also be implemented, because the success of extended enterprises is contingent on all members succeeding. An excellent case study is provided by the Boeing Company's 767 aircraft realization program of the late 1970s through early 1980s.

Improvement and Change Management

Enterprises competitive today generally will not be competitive tomorrow without a sustained concerted effort. A key to competitiveness is to consciously seek to improve, on a continuing basis, as an in-built element of all activities and processes.

Improvement comes with learning, and best-practice enterprises are continuously learning organizations. They learn from their own experiences and from the experience and knowledge of those around them. Knowledge management processes and supporting tools are used to capture information and lessons and leverage them across the enterprise.

Research and development activities contribute new ideas about technology and applications. Watchgroups monitor technological, competitive, governmental, financial, and societal horizons for changes. Processes for suggesting, evaluating, implementing, and rewarding improvement are embedded in the very fabric of the enterprise. Sharing knowledge is valued as a personal and corporate strength.

As has often been stated, change is the only constant. Agile enterprises recognize this reality, anticipate change, and manage accordingly. They develop capabilities to detect the occurrence of change, rapidly perform impact assessments, quickly replan, and then implement the plan in reasoned fashion.

Nowhere is this more important than in relation to product management. As customers come and go, orders arrive or are cancelled, new products are introduced and obsolete ones discontinued, the enterprise must be able to quickly react to such changes. Refer to Figure 5.11 for the iterative pattern of change and continuous improvement over a product's life cycle.

It is essential that a holistic, integrated approach be taken to the management of the product portfolio, enterprise operations, metrics, and resources in order to preclude the occurrence of suboptimization by the various functional organizations at the expense of the enterprise.

The product portfolio is managed at the enterprise level to ensure desired market coverage is achieved while precluding various organizational factions from developing redundant products, duplicating or overlapping market coverage, and reinventing technology and components unnecessarily. Marketing, engineering, manufacturing, and support operations are jointly optimized — together with the metrics used to measure their performance and determine their status — to prevent each functional area from suboptimizing, or even working at cross purposes, to the detriment of the enterprise as a whole.

Optimization must extend all the way down to the level of detailed plant and office functions to preclude disconnects from occurring between levels in the enterprise. For example, if the chosen strategic direction is one of increasing production and this is not effectively communicated below the plant or office manager level, then the implementation people may be focused on, for example, cost reduction measures that adversely impact the realization of increased production.

Change introduces risk. Whether the change is a process change, an innovation, the use of a new supplier, a new design, or the introduction of new technology, the successful enterprise proactively manages both the change itself and the resulting risk.

Lean and agile enterprises often need to assimilate technology changes out of competitive necessity, because of a loss of the supplier base, or for some other reason. Best-practice enterprises competing in the commercial business environment — where time-to-market is critical — adopt a technology management strategy that minimizes associated risk. This strategy dictates that only technology that is already reduced to practice and has been demonstrated to be producible in adequate volumes at acceptable rates may be considered for use in a product program. New technology, regardless of how desirable it may be from certain narrowly defined perspectives, is not considered for use until it reaches the foregoing level of maturity.

One consequence of this restrictive approach to technology change is that technology development must occur well upstream of the time at which it is to be used. It must also be fully developed, including proof that it can be manufactured. In cases where events force adoption of a technology change without benefit of the above strategy, the program that implements the change must recognize that a commensurate increase in risk is being incurred.

Many enterprises identify ways in which improvements may be made in the detailed processes extant at the worker level. Some enterprises recognize the importance of optimizing the next-higher-level process in which the workers are embedded. A few may even appreciate the fact that these low-level improvements, while significant, don't seem to be addressing whatever is causing the enterprise to lose its competitive edge. Only the rare, truly enlightened enterprise understands that it is only through total, integrated, top-down, and systematic optimization of all levels and facets of the value adding process that the largest improvements may be derived (see Figure 5.17).

An example of the limited understanding prevalent in American industrial enterprises is provided by a particular, but unnamed subassembly

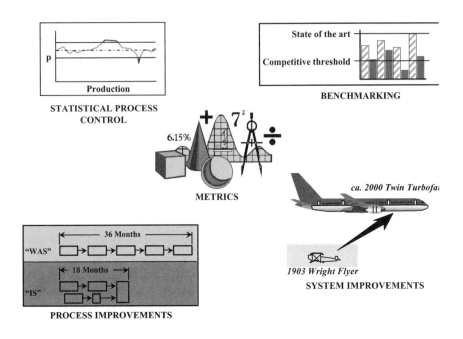

Figure 5.17 Continuous Improvement Techniques. A variety of total quality management tools and techniques are used in a conscientious program of error detection and elimination.

manufacturing plant. In this plant, achieving commanded production rates is sacrosanct. Nothing else truly matters. Improvements, while greatly needed and readily identifiable and even, sometimes, supported by internal plant funding, are generally not implementable due to the disruption they would impose on production rates. If and when they are even considered at all, they are limited to detail-level changes in workstation-specific machines, software, and operations.

As a consequence, customers are threatening to walk away due to poor quality. Reject rates are unacceptably high. Actual output is a mere fraction of targets. Employee morale is low and the personnel turnover rate is high. Management is imposing unwelcome attention, and other untoward things are occurring. No chance exists of curing the previously described symptoms in this plant because no possibility exists of effecting needed changes across a sufficient breadth or depth of this enterprise. This enterprise does not have improvement and change management processes in place.

The lean, agile enterprise establishes and uses metrics, benchmarking, and a total quality management (TQM) program as principal means of objectively assessing performance, identifying needed improvements, setting improvement goals, and tracking progress. The continuously learning enterprise stays competitive through concerted efforts to continuously improve systems, products, and all facets of the value-adding processes.

Processes are assessed and improved in two senses. Modern techniques, tools, and skills are suggested and implemented to replace less efficient ones — that is, state of the practice is one dimension of process. The other dimension of process is maturity. Familiar processes, supported by robust, reusable tools, allow employees to move from program to program and organization to organization without a loss of productivity. When metrics are added to processes, rates and efficiencies can be determined. With metrics, suggestions for improvements can be piloted and quantifiably evaluated. Changes and improvements move from being fads and buzzwords to meaningful additions to the bottom line. Savings are shared with those who suggest and implement improvements to encourage and reward employee participation in change improvement.

The process and metric maturity model in Figure 5.18 affords one objective measure of a learning enterprise environment.

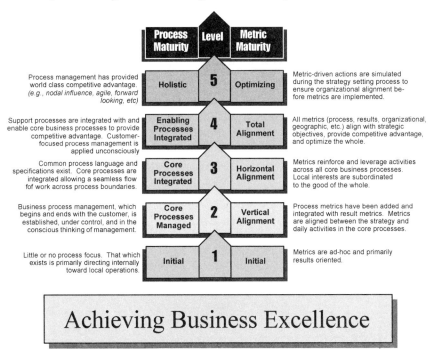

Capability Maturity and Improvement

Process Maturity	Level	Metric Maturity
Process management has provided world class competitive advantage. *(e.g., nodal influence, agile, forward looking, etc)*	**Holistic** — **5** — **Optimizing**	Metric-driven actions are simulated during the strategy setting process to ensure organizational alignment before metrics are implemented.
Support processes are integrated with and enable core business processes to provide competitive advantage. Customer-focused process management is applied unconsciously	**Enabling Processes Integrated** — **4** — **Total Alignment**	All metrics (process, results, organizational, geographic, etc.) align with strategic objectives, provide competitive advantage, and optimize the whole.
Common process language and specifications exist. Core processes are integrated allowing a seamless flow fof work across process boundaries.	**Core Processes Integrated** — **3** — **Horizontal Alignment**	Metrics reinforce and leverage activities across all core business processes. Local interests are subordinated to the good of the whole.
Business process management, which begins and ends with the customer, is established, under control, and in the conscious thinking of management.	**Core Processes Managed** — **2** — **Vertical Alignment**	Process metrics have been added and integrated with result metrics. Metrics are aligned between the strategy and daily activities in the core processes.
Little or no process focus. That which exists is primarily directing internally toward local operations.	**Initial** — **1** — **Initial**	Metrics are ad-hoc and primarily results oriented.

Achieving Business Excellence

Figure 5.18   Process and Metric Maturity. Continuously learning enterprises attain and sustain the fifth level of maturity.

Chapter 6

Implementing Best-Practice Enterprise

The realization of an integrated enterprise calls for several enabling initiatives, both technical and cultural. Clearly, an integrated system of information technologies is essential for quickly and accurately exchanging data within the extended enterprise. However, even more important are the initiatives that allow the organizations within the extended enterprise to create, exploit, and act upon information with a unity of purpose and to mutual benefit.

The first section in this chapter provides a generic model for implementing improvement within any enterprise. Evolving to a TIE is a journey of many steps. While operating the enterprise, there is a need to create improvement implementation activities and teams that will create the solutions that will eventually become the new operating procedures of the enterprise. As a way of understanding and prioritizing improvements, and as a method for driving technical requirements with business requirements, enterprise modeling is examined as a promising best practice for modern enterprise.

The next section provides two case studies on change implementation. The insights gained by others are appropriate for all practitioners of business.

The section on current initiatives and relationships presents three over-arching goals for any enterprise seeking to become agile and lean — adoption of integrated product management, development of robust enter-prise components for a flexible enterprise architecture, and the emergence of a learning organization. For each of the three objectives, a fishbone chart is used to show the key enablers and capabilities that influence its outcome.

Method for Implementing Improvement

Successfully implementing change and improvements within an enterprise is an enterprise best practice in itself. There are numerous models for managing change, but nearly all are characterized by four significant phases. The first phase is one of discovery — opportunities or calamities present themselves to enterprises that must then ponder their meaning and consequences. The second phase of implementing change is typically a time of making decisions. Good decisions, however, are best announced after analysis and as a set of actionable requirements for change. Often this phase is referred as the requirements phase.

Once requirements are established (that is, the problem to be solved is announced), the third phase creates potential solutions, selects the most promising one, proves that the answer, in fact, works, and prepares the way for deployment into the mainstream enterprise. The fourth phase is the real implementation of the fix throughout the enterprise and validating that the gains are holding. The bottom row of arrows across Figure 6.1 suggests such a process for implementing improvements.

One of the most perplexing problems for business leaders today is to know when a proposed solution is good. There are more than enough vendors and salespeople to assure you that everything will be just fine, but wouldn't it be nice to have a way of knowing just what your needs are before judging the correctness of the answer. The right solution to the wrong problem really is no bargain.

Business leaders need a way to effectively predict the effects of change and make a business case before incurring the cost and effort of change implementation. Enterprise modeling (EM) is a technique for analyzing business relationships, interactions, responsibilities, and desired results. Modern EM tools provide real leverage. Not only do they capture models and allow updates easily, they provide additional capability to simulate the proposed processes and estimate the effects. In a matter of weeks, business leaders can identify and assess the impact of potential changes before the decision is made to physically modify processes and systems.

At the same time, EM begins an integrated process for actually imple-menting improvements. As shown in Figure 6.1, EM starts with lessons from today's business and ends with specific requirements for changes

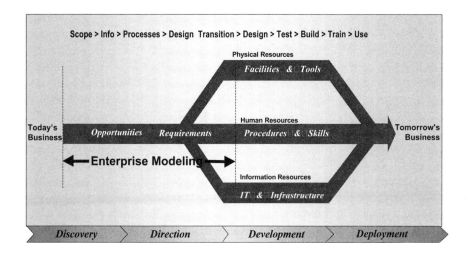

Figure 6.1   Enterprise Modeling in Improvement Implementation. Enterprise modeling is an emergent best practice used to determine and specify business requirements that drive the technical solutions required for enterprise improvement.

leading to tomorrow's business. The requirements may be for changes in the physical plant or tooling of a business, in the way people do work, or in automated information systems. More than likely, changes in all three areas are needed to fully realize new business opportunities.

Modern EM tools also provide easy transitions to development activities. Report generators provide easy-to-read requirements documents. Additional capabilities are provided by some toolmakers. Information attributes in the enterprise models can be loaded into database analyzers and automated design tools. Output from the data design tool can then be loaded into automated code generators, providing an end-to-end process for implementing change (at least within the IT domain).

EM depends on involvement and commitment from business leaders. The most important EM role is that of executive sponsor. The sponsor champions the need for improvement, provides strategic direction, authorizes and empowers resources, and then challenges the expert team to find creative and innovative solutions to selected problem areas. Current and recent managers form an expert team that defines the business scope, operations, events, triggers, rules, and results.

Business, not technical, language is used during modeling activities. Business attributes (headcount, cost, duration, etc.) can be captured as part of the requirements. Supplier, customer, and competitor relationships are mapped into the business flow. Internal processes, roles, and control sequences are identified. EM reflects everyday business objects (purchase orders, drawings, bills of material, shipping instructions, etc.) and activities (reviews, design, scheduling, production, billing, etc.).

One-for-one correspondence with real-world objects and actions makes the models intuitive and easily understandable. This allows business decision-makers to review proposed changes in nontechnical terms.

Modeling activities are coordinated by a project leader but conducted by a facilitator with a neutral role in defining requirements. The facilitator is assisted by a modeler/analyst who records the experts' output and translates it into various models that are readily understood by the development teams and by the expert team, after a little familiarization. IT and process developers are present during modeling, but they are basically listeners. They may answer questions about current capabilities, but they are there mostly to learn the reasons for the requirements that drive their systems and processes.

One common perception is that EM means creating one giant model of the whole business. There is considerable merit in doing a high-level, strategic, enterprise-wide model to identify areas of opportunity for improvement, but EM also works for selected subsets of the business.

EM is often performed incrementally for specific business areas in need of analysis and improvement. Each business area begins by placing itself into the overall enterprise context. Even though the focus is on one business domain, the enterprise perspective is preserved. Limiting the scope makes each project manageable and affordable. Fewer resources are needed and results are much timelier. A smaller step, with fast, tangible results, lends organizational credibility to EM and reinforces its desirability as a best-practice skill.

The ultimate form of credibility, of course, is when the improvement continuously adds to the bottom line. Modeling is not an end unto itself; it's a tool for making decisions. Done properly, modeling is an investment — it pays its own way.

Each EM project has well-established phases, each with discrete deliverables that feed the next steps. As suggested by the top row in Figure 6.1, the project phases are intended to scope the area of improvement, capture the information and process requirements from the business perspective, and effect a smooth translation of business requirements into technical performance requirements and preliminary designs. The consistency and repeatability of the modeling activities make EM a skill that is not difficult to master. The first projects may cause participants to learn some new tricks, but as the activities become familiar and participants trust the process, projects tend to move faster and improvements become more focused. Doing EM routinely to analyze and assess potential changes should become an essential part of any continuous improvement process.

After an enterprise modeling project is complete, a design and development project is launched as the next step in improvement implementation.

There are numerous lean and six-sigma type initiatives and processes available, which use cross-functional teams to find root-cause problems and create innovative solutions for solving them. One important aspect of designing solutions involves designing the training that will be needed for personnel to use any new procedures or tools.

After the selected solution and the deployment methods have been validated, typically in small pilot projects, the enterprise enters into the third and final phase of implementation. Deployment of new tools and processes may be on a wholesale basis, but often, the introduction of change must be incremental. Rather than stop the existing processes and programs cold, make changes, and then try to regain lost production and momentum, it is often more practical to introduce changes at naturally occurring break points in product program execution. In large corporations with multiple products and product lines, the full implementation of one change may take several months if not years. While a full discussion of this topic is a bit beyond scope, it should be recognized that the implementation of change is a vital and often underrated task in improvement.

Case Studies

The following two cases come to mind in recognizing the need for a totally integrated enterprise perspective. These represent two different aspects of integrating work and/or information within an enterprise. Success can be measured differently based on the activity undertaken. In the business world success is measured in currency. Establishing metrics and ensuring that they support the strategic and tactical business requirements will always provide a competitive edge.

Case One: A Great Idea, But, ...

Business: Automobile manufacturer
Project Objective: Integrating business, engineering, and manufacturing information
Creating an integrated information environment where business, engineering, and manufacturing information are interrelated is an enormous undertaking. Few companies have been successful in their first attempts and/or

their successes have been less than desired. Understanding how the information synchronizes the business strategies is often lacking and as such only the data is integrated, not the information.

In this case, three years were spent defining the requirements, modeling the problems and developing the application. The application created an extended ERP (enterprise resource planning) environment separately for each division of the company. This allowed the linkage of warranty, financial, customer requirements, product requirements, engineering, and manufacturing within each division. It also allowed the sharing of some information across divisions.

A rapid application development process was utilized to cause incremental roll-outs and provide early user feedback. Initially everyone was impressed with the potential for the project, and as it was rolled out to the individual divisions certain parts of the application became popular with the users and managers. The champions of the project were individually congratulated by their specific divisions.

After installation and training it became obvious that each division was utilizing only some of the application's capability. In retrospect, the utilization rate for the application was less than anyone would have expected. With the exception of specific portions of the application, that were sponsored by their own division's champion, everyone preferred to use their own applications or systems.

Why? It was a great idea. The application provided superior information availability! It turns out that with each division being its own profit center, and information technology budgets being held at the corporate level, and common systems being the theme of the day, that each champion really needed some aspect of the application and found this application development activity a way to fund them.

Each division had approved the data models and entity definitions and assumed that there would be no problem in implementing the complete application and at the same time they would have their specific needs met. What was not understood was that each division had their own processes and the users could not move to a new application or system that did not encompass their particular processes.

In the months that followed it was evident that for each division to map their processes to the new application was a cost that was not expected and that certainly the application would have to be changed to accommodate these common processes. As a result only pieces of this application are in use today.

I'm sure I don't have to explain where all the wrong decisions were made here but, one aspect requires repeating: understand that business strategies mapped to product/process development processes is a necessity before buying or creating an information technology solution.

Case Two: Mistaken Identity

Business: Discrete parts manufacturer.

Project Objective: Create a sales management database to track, associate, and sort multiple customers and multiple saleable parts

Associating parts to clients, clients to parts and dollars seemed easy. The responsible sales and marketing director decided to implement a customer relationship management (CRM) system. The sales and marketing requirements were defined, a CRM market analysis was conducted, and a vendor chosen. The CRM system was installed in less than two months. This is remarkable and was due primarily to the sales and marketing director. His team had nailed the requirements and selected a super vendor. All of the sales and marketing representatives underwent training, and when the switch was thrown the new system performed as expected by the director and his team.

Let's move 30 days into the future from when the new CRM system came online. It turns out that not all the requirements were understood. Supporting systems for project management, engineering, and manufacturing were no longer providing needed information.

Consider other requirements. When you have over 10,000 current parts and 600 new projects, it becomes required to integrate sales, engineering, project management, and manufacturing. Not to include or understand the dependencies of the other areas of the business in terms of CRM information is suicide. It is not as simple as installing a CRM system. Engineering resources and plant capacities are analyzed in conjunction with new sales. Plans for launching new products depend on more than just the salesperson's making a sale. The business had to return to its old system. It had mistakenly identified a problem that could not be solved without understanding processes beyond the realm of sales and marketing.

As it turns out, the problems resulting from this lack of planning and understanding caused the business to analyze its information technology requirements in terms of the overall needs. It started with the strategic analysis of its goals and considered its resources (people, facilities, technology) before establishing a team to create an enterprise model that illustrated the many diverse needs of the different functional areas.

Current Initiatives and Relationships

Creating and sustaining an agile enterprise requires that the entire organization comprehends and thrives on change.

> Change is the only constant in modern business, and only those enterprises with people, processes, and resources that understand, detect, adapt to, and prosper with change will survive in the intensely competitive manufacturing arena.

Understanding the integrated product management and using IPTs to execute product and service development are essential for detecting change in markets and customers. Starting with the voices of the customers and ending with the customers' assessment of how well the product performed over its useful life keeps an enterprise attuned to the needs and priorities of the marketplace. Including customers and suppliers in the IPTs keeps product development on target — both in terms of shifting customer priorities and adjusting to changes in the suppliers' capabilities to deliver their portions of the product.

The creation of robust, reusable enterprise components is key to the ability to deal with and exploit change. Tightly cohesive, loosely coupled modules of enterprise functionality are designed with change in mind. One persistent goal is the development of intelligent, open architecture modules with components that anticipate a range of conditions, imperfect inputs, and the need to be revised quickly and often. Rigorous interfaces for the modules allow the enterprise to plug and play the functional components — a mark of a truly agile enterprise. Finally, enterprise modeling (based on the components) provides an analytical capability to propose and simulate multiple responses to change — this capability is the one that allows enterprises to truly exploit change, rather than merely survive it.

If change is constant, then it becomes imperative that the enterprise culture values and rewards the new while retaining the strength of the proven past. The information management resources must in be place to allow individual members of the organization to access and use knowledge already learned by the group. This requires subject matter experts to manage the knowledge content for completeness, accuracy, and currency. Process owners are required to design methods and tools that leverage knowledge and then to deploy and improve the processes and tools. Teachers and mentors are required to help newer members of the organization learn what is available, how to use it to an advantage, and how to contribute to the knowledge base. Technical and organizational intelligence is required, about both the internal enterprise and the potential competition. Research is required to identify and apply new technology and knowledge for continued competitive advantage. A pervasive desire for improvement is a palpable attribute of world-class agile manufacturers.

Integrated Product Management

The successful execution of product programs, based on the total-life-cycle concept of IPPD, is the fundamental core of the enterprise. Competent people, processes, and resources — focused on the customer's needs and the products that will satisfy them — are brought together in the notion of an enterprise that launches one successful IPPD effort after another.

In order to execute parallel product programs, each using an IPPD methodology, the enterprise must first have a portfolio — an arrangement of products, resources, and finances over a strategic planning window. The portfolio identifies and creates the high-level business objectives for product programs. Understanding the portfolio and implementing the business development processes that create it are critical for establishing fair and feasible contracts between the IPTs and the enterprise.

In order to execute integrated product management, a common process for integrated product development must be in place for the enterprise, and a generic product development process must be in place for each major product line. Guidelines and criteria for product- and customer-specific tailoring should also be available. Each current program should be consistent with level resource allocation and nonoverlapped phasing of activities. This notion of cadence prevents all product programs from demanding the same people, facilities, and support at the same time.

One key enabler for steady cadence is common and repeatable pro-cesses for each product program. IPPD is a best practice for product life-cycle development and management. Repeated processes, taking about the same amount of time, allow an enterprise to determine resources levels that are steady-state. Anyone who has had to do massive hiring for a demand spike, and then had to go through equally massive layoffs when the demand inevitably fades, can appreciate the significance of common process and predictable schedules.

The common IPPD process and all subsequent process models must have been analyzed and tailored to provide a lean value stream for customer satisfaction. Value-added process steps and best-implementation techniques and tools must be identified and integrated into the enterprise's operating components. Innovation teams are formed to examine specific product lines and operations; using a structured change management process, these teams pilot and then roll-out the best lean practices for the enterprise.

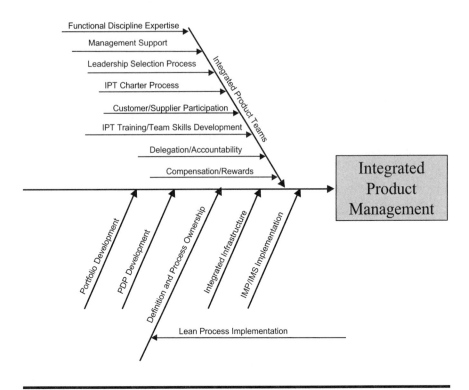

Figure 6.2 Influence Diagram for Integrated Product Management. Integrated product teams and mastery of core processes (core competencies) are the most vital steps for executing multiple IPPD-based product teams simultaneously.

Pivotal to the success of IPPD is an information infrastructure that lets the cross-functional teams execute lean processes and make timely decisions based on a virtual, unified body of information designed to support the IPPD process (see Figure 6.2).

Successful execution of IPPD-based programs requires the implementation of integrated master plans and integrated master schedules. Each program must have its IMP and IMS, and all the IMP/IMS collectively must align with and support the enterprise portfolio.

The key enabler for IPPD-based programs is the implementation of IPTs. Without people trained in the mechanics of the IPPD and the dynamics of team development, the adaptation of all other initiatives is effectively negated. All other initiatives are designed to make teams of people more effective and efficient — if the teams don't know what to do or how to act, little is gained over the current enterprise approaches.

The implementation of IPTs requires substantial work in creating a culture that can create, sustain, and reward successful IPTs. The execution of IPPD-based programs as an enterprise core competency requires substantial development and training in lean engineering and manufacturing processes and empowered, cross-functional teams.

Robust Enterprise Components and Flexible Architecture

Agile enterprise is an end, not a means. The awareness of, and readiness for, change is something that must be designed and built into every part of the enterprise. Sturdy, reusable pieces of enterprise that can be easily and quickly disconnected and reconnected are the building-block components. Flexible, adaptive connectors allow the enterprise to respond to change (reconfigure) with a minimum of effort and disruption.

The first enabler for flexible enterprise architecture is a component-based strategy. The enterprise must accept that what it is today is not what it needs to be tomorrow. It also learns to value highly adaptable pieces of enterprise, not the glorious (but ephemeral) totality of the enterprise structure. Fundamentally, this requires a shift in organizational philosophy — multilayered management needs to be flattened. Control from the top is replaced with orchestration and facilitation. Value-adding enterprise components must be empowered to act quickly and efficiently — so long as they fulfill the terms of their charter (contract) with the overall enterprise. Decisions are made at the lowest possible level of activity by teams fully aware of its expectations.

A robust enterprise component is an element of the business that has the ability to adjust easily to variability in its input and still create its expected output. A robust component remains functional (and can be reused) as long as the essential purpose of the element is the same relative to the enterprise. The basic enabler for robust components is the conscientious and deliberate design of business elements that comprehend the principles of variability and cohesion. Variability in the volume of input is accommodated by component scalability. Variability in the range of input is accommodated by designed-in bandwidth. Built-in validation, smoothing, and default provisions accommodate variability in the quality of input.

A robust component is typically a simple component. It performs one basic function, or a tightly coupled (cohesive) set of subfunctions, and requires no awareness of why or how it is being used in the larger context.

It acts only on the input it is given and with the intelligence designed into it. Inherently, low-level components are more robust than high-level ones because of the simplicity of scope. Robust (complex) components at higher levels can be designed if stable business rules are added to the element's intelligence and the input set is expanded to include adequate control. Smart systems and intelligent agents are enabling best practices for robust, complex components.

With robust components available, flexible enterprise architectures become possible — as long as the ability to easily connect, disconnect, and reconnect the components is in place. The primary enablers for component interoperability are well-defined, stable (i.e., formal) interfaces. Formal interfaces are a natural extension of stable, robust components. Even if the component changes internally (for improved performance or cost), as long as the required inputs and the expected outputs remain the same, the enterprise is unaffected. The impact of direct interface changes is substantial. Not only must the processing component change, but all other components that potentially interact with it must change. The role of each component and how it fits into the overall enterprise value stream must be well understood in order to create stable interfaces. The key enabler for this aspect is enterprise information and data design — enterprise data models are used to capture the business requirements and are then translated into the actual data and material that moves through the enterprise channels.

Components with well-defined interfaces can be leveraged to achieve virtual, distributed enterprises. Since the components are no longer directly connected, but connected by pipes — the distributed enterprise is enabled by lengthening the pipes. Clearly, the pipes must be big enough to move data and material through the enterprise fast enough; but the reality of the enterprise design is that a pipe is also an enterprise component, and it, too, can be designed to be robust and flexible.

Distributed, virtual enterprises are also enabled by two vital initiatives: interoperability infrastructure and standardization. Well-defined interfaces are not necessarily directly connectable. Take real pipes used in household plumbing as an example. Pipes of different diameters (each widely available and often used) are joined by an adapter; two abutting threaded ends can be coupled by a sleeve; pipes meeting from different directions can be joined by an elbow — sometimes, changes in direction and size are accommodated simultaneously.

Disparate enterprise data can be integrated through the implementation of adapter/connector middleware, and this is the preferred practice where large amounts of legacy capability is still viable. However, over the longer term, as new enterprise components are designed and implemented, standard interfaces and pipes are the best practice. Over time, the goal is to reduce the need for elaborate adaptation parts by using well-defined, directly connectable components.

One of the inherited difficulties of distributed enterprise is the vulnerability of the enterprise to disruption. Agile enterprise creates interdependencies among the enterprise components and the links that join them. Loss of a vital function or link potentially means the entire enterprise is disabled. In addition to traditional security measures that attempt to harden each element and link, and make them inaccessible to anyone other than authorized users, there is an emerging best practice called survivable systems. Survivable systems assume that one or more of the enterprise components will at some time or another be compromised. Additional security attributes are designed into the components and the system to detect an intrusion and to dynamically reconfigure into an alternative (degraded) mode that keeps the critical functions of the system working in some fashion.

Agile enterprises that seek to fully exploit change as a competitive advantage create an enterprise simulation capability. Rather than wait for change to be forced on it, the agile enterprise uses an enterprise simulator to analyze what-if scenarios (see Figure 6.3). The enterprise data models created by the information engineering activity are inserted into a simulator. Business rules are also inserted. Organizational dynamics are emulated. A flight simulator is used to create abnormal conditions to train

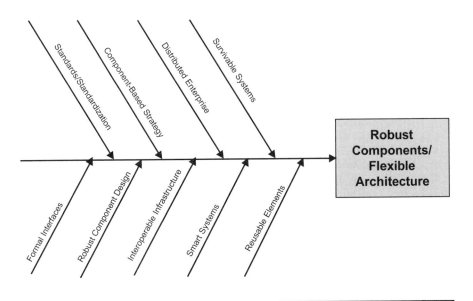

Figure 6.3   Influence Diagram for Robust Enterprise Components. Components are designed to readily adapt to change to make restructuring and optimizing the enterprise easier.

pilots and improve flight procedures. By analogy, an enterprise simulator is used by the executive management and business developers to prepare for change and improve enterprise procedures. The same simulator is used to analyze changes proposed from within the enterprise by the continuous improvement process to order to prevent local optimization from degrading the overall enterprise performance.

Learning Organizations

Agile enterprises stay agile only by learning quickly and efficiently, by integrating lessons into the collective wisdom of the enterprise, and by making the wisdom globally accessible and usable by all enterprise elements. When knowledge of new capabilities and tools surfaces, learning organizations inject technology in deliberate fashion — considering the overall business needs and the impact on product portfolio.

Transformation into a learning organization is the ultimate measure of an agile enterprise. An enterprise changes because it (a) must, (b) can, or (c) wants to. An enterprise forced into change does so grudgingly, with minimal expectations, and hopes never to suffer that agony again — only to be overwhelmed by the next change the competition forces on it. An enterprise that changes simply because it can may be a fun place to work, but it is a serendipitous adventure. Implementing change requires significant time, money, and effort: without knowing whether the expenditure adds value to the enterprise, how can a change for the sake of change be deemed anything but foolish?

A learning enterprise understands that change is inevitable. While it knows there is always some danger in making changes, it also understands that nothing is perfect; every change is an opportunity for improvement. The learning enterprise makes changes because it wants to. A proactive attitude about continuous improvement must be ingrained within the organizational culture. The learning organization has highly sensitive internal and external antennae and market, product, and business indicators are constantly measured and analyzed for trends and deviations. Spotting an opportunity first and being able to change easily to exploit it are items that agile entrepreneurial dreams are made of. The learning organization also has a robust communication plan and a network for communicating change.

Once the mindset is in place, an enterprise needs several other enablers to become a learning organization. Knowledge, like any other element, must add value to the enterprise. The processes in the customer value stream, and the enabling and support processes, define the knowledge domains and the levels of expertise required by the enterprise; because of this, process owners are key enablers for learning. Process owners are also responsible for continuous improvement of the enterprise processes and the knowledge that supports them. A process for continuous improvement is an enabler that allows everyone in the enterprise to participate in a disciplined method for identifying and implementing better ideas, techniques, and tools within the enterprise.

Subject-matter experts support process owners. Experts tend to the currency, accuracy, and accumulation of knowledge; process owners ensure the knowledge is accessed and used in the enterprise activities. The experts are also logical candidates for mentors; they possess the deep subject knowledge to nurture those less familiar; but mentoring requires its own skills, and the experts may require training in communication and coaching.

Knowledge management and knowledge tools are best-practice enablers for leveraging the collective learning of an enterprise. Lessons learned the hard way should be learned just once. Success stories should become preferred practice. The processes and tools for getting each person and organization in the enterprise to contribute to and draw from the corporate memory must be implemented throughout the enterprise in order to become a learning organization.

Knowledge may be gained coincidentally or deliberately. Learning organizations accommodate coincidental knowledge, but more importantly, they proactively seek the kinds of information and knowledge vital to sustaining the agile enterprise. Research and development capabilities are fundamental enablers for advancing knowledge internally. Learning organizations also seek knowledge from external sources as well. One critical source of knowledge for a competitive enterprise is the competition itself. Continual studies of the industry's benchmarks and analysis of the trends are key activities for the learning organization.

When new knowledge suggests that new technology needs to be brought into the enterprise — either as a product enhancement or an enhancement to the enterprise's core or enabling resources — a well-conceived plan for nondisruptive insertion must be executed. A technical injection process and the training capability implied are key learning enablers.

The overarching enabler for continuous learning is, of course, a body of enlightened employees. The idea of sharing information may be either threatening or rewarding, depending on the enterprise's cultural values.

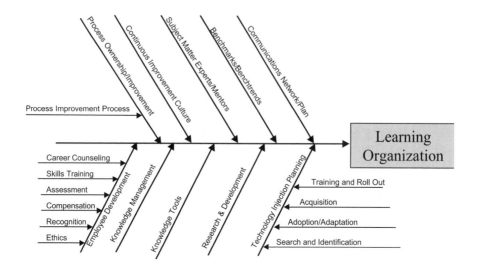

Figure 6.4 Influence Diagram for a Learning Organization. An agile enterprise can remain agile only as long as the enterprise can detect and manage change. A learning organization is predicated on the notion that the best way to spot and respond to change is to constantly acquire and share information in order to improve the enterprise.

The old notion of making oneself indispensable by being the only source of information must be replaced by a sense of delight in sharing insight with others and, in turn, growing exponentially when others share their learning. Identifying the skills and proficiency levels needed by enterprise; creating the means for employees to assess their competencies; mutual planning for personal and professional growth; creating the ethos, compensation, and rewards for information sharing — these are all parts of employee development that enable the learning enterprise (see Figure 6.4).

Innovation Trends

Industry study groups provide trend predictions for the next several years. Incorporating their vision into the implementation planning for TIE saves invention and duplication of effort.

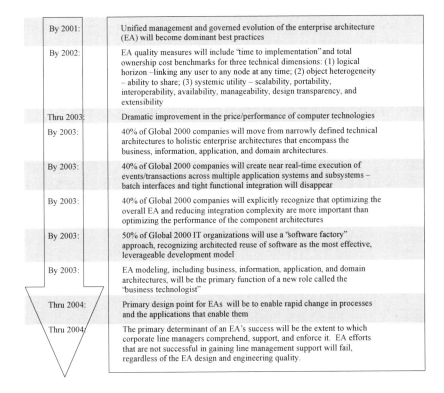

By 2001:	Unified management and governed evolution of the enterprise architecture (EA) will become dominant best practices
By 2002:	EA quality measures will include 'time to implementation" and total ownership cost benchmarks for three technical dimensions: (1) logical horizon –linking any user to any node at any time; (2) object heterogeneity – ability to share; (3) systemic utility – scalability, portability, interoperability, availability, manageability, design transparency, and extensibility
Thru 2003:	Dramatic improvement in the price/performance of computer technologies
By 2003:	40% of Global 2000 companies will move from narrowly defined technical architectures to holistic enterprise architectures that encompass the business, information, application, and domain architectures.
By 2003:	40% of Global 2000 companies will create near real-time execution of events/transactions across multiple application systems and subsystems – batch interfaces and tight functional integration will disappear
By 2003:	40% of Global 2000 companies will explicitly recognize that optimizing the overall EA and reducing integration complexity are more important than optimizing the performance of the component architectures
By 2003:	50% of Global 2000 IT organizations will use a 'software factory" approach, recognizing architected reuse of software as the most effective, leverageable development model
By 2003:	EA modeling, including business, information, application, and domain architectures, will be the primary function of a new role called the 'business technologist"
Thru 2004:	Primary design point for EAs will be to enable rapid change in processes and the applications that enable them
Thru 2004:	The primary determinant of an EA's success will be the extent to which corporate line managers comprehend, support, and enforce it. EA efforts that are not successful in gaining line management support will fail, regardless of the EA design and engineering quality.

Figure 6.5   IT Innovation Trends. Advances in information technology will be fast enough to afford ample opportunities for enterprise improvement — if the enterprise's culture in ready to accept the management style changes required to take advantage of information revolution.

Several services and groups annually provide predictions of IT trends. Figure 6.5 illustrates some trends that we have come to believe are in the forefront when looking at TIE. Several of the major themes in the enterprise architecture strategy are of particular interest:

- The next technical steps will unify management and emphasize total (extended) enterprise connectivity and interoperability.
- Major efforts on enterprise architecture will be made toward the ability to evolve and handle rapid change.
- The price and performance of computer technology will continue to dramatically improve.
- Reusability and optimized architectures (not components) will be the hallmarks of agile enterprise — business technologists will use enterprise modeling to plan change.

■ Enterprise architectures that do not gain line management support will fail regardless of the enterprise architecture design and engineering quality.

Figure 6.5 provides a summary and timeline of the 10 most significant trends for the years 2001 to 2004. The table is arranged by calendar year. A most significant finding (i.e., the only trend that uses the word fail) is that without changing the management style, from the top through the line supervisor level, efforts at improving the enterprise architecture will return very little gain.

Appendix A:
List of Acronyms
and Abbreviations

API	application program(mer) interface
BMPCoE	Best Manufacturing Practices Center of Excellence
CAD	computer-aided design
CAE	computer-aided engineering
CAIV	cost as an independent variable
CAM	computer-aided manufacturing
CoE	center(s) of excellence
DoD	Department of Defense
DW	data warehousing
EA	enterprise architecture
FEOTB	forward edge of the business
HR	human resources
IDEF0	Integration DEFinition language 0
IOC	Industrial Operations Command
IPPD	integrated product and process development
IPD	integrated product development
IPT	integrated product team(s)
IS	information system(s)
IT	information technology
JIT	just-in-time
ODS	operational data store(s)
PDP	product development process

RFP   request for proposal
RFQ   request for quotation
TQM   total quality management
WBS   work breakdown structure

Appendix B: Glossary of Operational Definitions

Advertising push: Use of advertising to make something visible in the marketplace with the hope of attracting customers.

Autonomous function: A function that is able to execute successfully with only the inputs provided, without depending on the state of other enterprise components.

Benchmark(ing): To determine a state or characterize something for use in making comparisons, achieving definition, or establishing a reference basis (e.g., capability or performance levels of a set of similar products offered by competing companies).

Business rule(s): Guidelines, requirements, definitions, relationships (including mathematical relationships), and interpretations that reflect, determine, model, or otherwise represent business considerations.

Champion(s): Individuals who initiate, defend, foster, and clear obstacles impeding an activity, program, or operation.

Continuous improvement: The philosophy and practice of improving, or making something better, on an ongoing basis.

Core: Fundamental, unique, and/or characteristic that an enterprise identifies as those things without which the enterprise loses its competitiveness identity or distinctiveness.

Core competency(-ies): The set of capabilities, experiences, facilities, strengths, expertise, employee talent, and related things that are sufficiently unique and valuable to distinguish one enterprise from another and that induce customers to choose one enterprise over another

Core processes: Proprietary processes that provide unique products (goods + services) that appeal to customers and thereby enable the enterprise to successfully compete.

Core resource(s): Those portions of the human, financial, and physical basis of operation that are unique and enable the enterprise to successfully complete product programs

Enterprise: A unit of economic organization or activity; especially a business organization.

Enterprise component: A process — together with its allocated resources — that has a clear and reusable function and that is capable of interacting with one or more other enterprise components across predefined interfaces and in accordance with business requirements.

Enterprise leadership: The processes, personnel, and resources concerned with the executive function of an enterprise.

Enterprise system: A perspective in which an enterprise is considered as a complex system.

Executable component(s): Defined processes — together with their allocated resources — that have clear and reusable functions that are capable of being repeatedly performed.

Extended enterprise: An abstract superset comprised of two or more enterprises.

Extended enterprise chain: An extended enterprise assuming a structure resembling a linked chain, hierarchy, or other ordered structure.

Flexible architecture: A design that allows modifications to be made to its (1) element interconnection structure, (2) functional structure — while remaining within the limits of the overall design.

Forward edge of the business: That business activity concerned with the acquisition of market information and new business.

Framework: (1) A reference system for describing and comparing enterprise architectures; (2) the foundations and skeletal structure of an architecture.

Functional block: A building block, component, or other entity that performs one or more functions.

Functional organization: An organization whose role and/or reason for being is to perform some function(s).

Generic architecture: A simplified, nonspecific structural design used as an abstraction, or as a model, of multiple structural designs (that may differ considerably when considered in specific detail), which embodies aspects common or otherwise applicable to the set of designs it represents.

High-level architecture: A structural design that embodies only the largest aspects, elements, or considerations of greatest import with respect to the entity under consideration.

IDEF0 Methodology: That approach, technique, or method of structured analysis, design, and modeling that utilizes, or is known as, IDEF0.

Interaction(s): Mutual or reciprocal actions or influences exerted by/on/among two or more things, whether directly or indirectly.

Interface(s): Any occurrence of a flow of something from one thing to another involving the crossing of the boundaries of the entities involved.

Kanban: A pull signal used to indicate that more material is required. A just-in-time manufacturing technique, a Kanban was originally a card placed near the end of a production lot — an operator, upon reaching the card, would place it in a position visible to material handlers who would bring the next lot of material to the operator's station, just in time.

Margin(s): $(100\,\%) \times [(\text{Product Selling Price}) - (\text{Product Cost})] / (\text{Product Cost})$.

Methodology: A body of procedures, rules, methods, and postulates employed by some discipline.

Metric(s): A standard or measure.

Shared Processes: Processes applicable to and usable in multiple contexts.

Simulation The modeling or representation of the dynamics of one system using another.

Unique processes: Processes that are not replicated or replicable outside the enterprise possessing them.

Validation: One or more of (1) inspection, (2) analysis, (3) demonstration, and (4) test, performed to verify requirements, designs, or product.

Appendix C: Bibliography

Acquisition Reform Office, Open Systems, in *The Virtual Town Hall Meetings*, 1997 and 1998, at Web site:
http://www.acq-ref.navy.mil/vth/opensystems.html.

Alter, S., *Information Systems*, 3rd ed., Addison-Wesley, Reading, MA, 1999.

American Productivity and Quality Center, *Process Classification Framework*.

Collis, D. J., and Montgomery, C. A., *Corporate Strategy, A Resource-Based Approach*; Irwin/McGraw-Hill, New York, 1998.

DoD Integrated Product and Process Development Handbook, Office of the Under Secretary of Defense (Acquisition and Technology), July 1998.

Inmon, W. H., *Corporate Information Factory*, John Wiley & Sons, Wiley Computer Publishing, New York, 1998.

Kerzner, H., *Project Management, A Systems Approach to Planning, Scheduling, and Controlling*, 6th ed., Van Nostrand Reinhold, New York, 1997.

META Group, *1999 Trends — Enterprise Architecture Strategies*, at Web site http://clients.metagroup.com.

Mish, F. C. et al., *Merriam Webster's Collegiate Dictionary*, 10th ed., Merriam-Webster Inc., Springfield, MA, 1996.

Appendix D: Information Technology Requirements

The information provided in this appendix is an example of requirement items to be used to derive further questions that would enable the selection of information technology for a totally integrated enterprise.

The following is a summary list illustrating requirements that should be questioned when evaluating technology or products for an enterprise application, system, or technical solution. Depending on the item being evaluated for selection, not all of them will apply. Also others may be added to the list as appropriate.

The following points of equal priority represent nontechnical highlights of the set of requirements that are common to all IT needs:

- Hardware and software solutions are appropriate and support industry standards and open architectures. This requires parallel and convergent solutions.
- Security is critical and must protect proprietary information of all elements of the enterprise.

- Flexibility in standard configurations must be available for RAM, disk size, and screen size to meet the task requirements.
- TCP/IP protocol with Web technology will be the strategic direction.
- The infrastructure must provide broad access to shared resources including peripherals, servers, and data.
- Data must maintain its information content as it moves through various processes and organizations.
- Current solution sets must evolve with technology, and a process for periodic refresh must be defined.

The sample IT requirements are structured under the following 12 major headings:

- Accessibility
- Application-Specific
- Backup, Archive, Restore
- Capacity
- Communication
- Compatibility
- Cost/Pricing
- Hardware/Ergonomics
- Performance
- Printing
- Security
- Support

Others may be added as appropriate. Careful consideration should always be given to any requirement to ensure that it is truly a requirement (a must-have to work) and not merely a preference (a want-to-have).

Accessibility

- Fully networked and interconnected environment allowing authorized access to all resources within a LAN or across the WAN
- Free and easy authorized access to engineering and business information and applications
- Ability to communicate, collaborate, and coordinate with internal and external resources
- Ability to exchange and translate data with other networked and e-mail systems, e.g., Telnet, file transfer protocol (FTP), NFS, Lotus Notes, and Internet SMTP mail

- Authorized access to data on remote as well as LAN-attached computers
- Supports video conferencing, multimedia applications, and write-capable CD-ROM

Application-Specific

- Support for large file sharing and access using standard industry protocols and tools (e.g., NFS, FTP)
- Compatibility with network support libraries
- Compatibility with standard X-Windows display emulation. Performance shall be at least 80% of server performance
- Access to the complete set of applications from a vendor product
- Access to mainframe (and services)
- User ability to cut and paste information between application views and retain native attributes of text and graphic information
- User ability to capture the full content and intention from what is seen on the screen and save this information in universally accepted formats to a file, the clipboard, or a printer
- Ability to compress electronically captured image files, both lossless and lossy, with industry-standard user-selectable amount of compression
- Universal availability of Microsoft personal productivity tools on PCs
- Operating systems support multiple applications running simultaneously and unrestricted by memory constraints of hardware or operating system
- Availability of code libraries that provide full access to the operating system
- Availability of programming language editors that are sensitive to the syntax of selected software like JAVA, C, C++, Lisp, and Visual Basic
- Provision for source code version control, examples include SCCS, RCS, PVCS, Visual Safe Source
- Ability to compress (and decompress) all file types, with or without including a self-expanding capability and multidisk spanning capability
- A consistent, industry-standard look and feel across all environments and applications, to facilitate access and information creation and sharing
- Systems support for group workflow management tools
- Ability to capture hardcopy images into universally accepted formats for inclusion into electronic media
- Support of configuration management tools

- Systems that provide software installation utilizing automatic discovery capability to identify differences in hardware configurations
- Easy, local user access to all system and application documentation, in online and/or hardcopy form (both if available), hyperlinked and searchable by keywords, context and full text search
- CAE, CAD, and CAM applications that support industry-standard graphics file formats for exchange
- Ability for system users to exchange usable design/drafting data files (100% of surface, solid, and drawing files)
- Users have sketch capability with ability to exchange files with existing design/drafting tools (e.g., AutoCAD), 3D functionality is desired
- Ability for desktop systems to exchange document facsimiles with fax facilities
- Ability to edit and annotate textual and graphical captured images
- Access to optical character recognition (OCR) software for creating textual data from electronic image capture files
- Support of standard browsers and multimedia authoring tools
- Ability to use groups and mailing lists to send files, e-mail, and faxes

Backup, Archive, and Restore

- Backup, archive, and restore services available for all desktop devices
- Time schedules for backup, archive, and restore dictated by local business needs
- Easy user access to backup, archive, and restore services
- Support for local backup and archive on user-controlled, industry-standard media, using a standard, full-featured application
- Backup and archiving systems that verify data integrity

Capacity

- Local management able to configure devices to meet local business needs

Communication

- Connectivity between computers provided by gateways and firewalls to the Internet
- Secure access to all primary functions and access to all authorized data from remote locations, e.g., encrypted connectivity via the global telephone system, both stationary and cellular

- TCP/IP communication protocol supported by all systems, with DECnet and IPX support as needed
- Use open and industry standards
- Ability to utilize Web to communicate data, applications, reports, etc.
- E-mail communications, including application-formatted attachments, compatible with Internet mail

Compatibility

- Accessibility of information contained in data files and on media developed on older versions of software applications and platforms when upgrades are made to applications or to the infrastructure. Long-term information integrity shall follow a declared policy.
- File integrity retained during data transfer over the network (to another computer or output device), i.e., no filtering of data unless documented
- Application software, display systems, and hardcopy output devices support standard document formats, for both display and hardcopy output, using industry-standard fonts (weight, typeface)
- Systems support for industry-standard graphics file formats
- Systems and applications support for industry-standard high-resolution digital color image file formats
- User-configurable and macro-capable keyboards with specific mapping for various emulators
- Nonproprietary system and bus designs that fully support industry standards for communication with add-in cards, drives, and peripherals

Cost Pricing

- Annual review of end-user requirements and their quantified impact on systems and support costs
- Competitive benchmarks for systems and services provided to meet user requirements

Hardware Ergonomics

- Network capability for all devices, plus standalone capability for portables
- Quick, secure, and reliable device connections

- Ergonomic design of all user devices, to meet requirements for display emissions and adjustability, standard keyboard layout with provision for cursor control using a mouse or trackball
- Capability to read data from a multiple devices (CD, DVD, ZIP, etc.)
- Availability (for all user systems) of removable nonvolatile storage using disk or, as appropriate, tape or other large data storage devices
- Standard systems I/O ports: one serial port (minimum, not counting mouse port); one parallel port (minimum); one 10/100 Base T port (minimum); SCSI and IEEE-488 optional
- Standard systems expansion options (desktop systems; minimum 2 slots; 6 slots optional)
- All output devices meet environmental standards for the area in which they are used
- Portable devices meet field weight requirements. Consideration should be given to including the following features. (1) Color screens that are adjustable to allow operating in direct sunlight. (2) Support of standard bus peripherals (SCSI) as well as expansion capabilities for PCMCIA, EISA, and ISA standards. (3) Portable batteries that provide 4 hours of operation without recharge and 8 hours with a spare battery
- Expandable nonvolatile storage space, local removable storage available as an option
- Desktop display (minimum) is a 17-inch diagonal display with 256 color, 1024 × 768 pixels resolution, and user-adjustable contrast and brightness

Performance

- Annual review of minimum RAM requirements
- Optional availability of floating-point processors and graphics accelerators
- Hardcopy printing over the network at 12 pages per minute, with locally attached printer speeds and features as required

Printing

- Industry-standard output file formats used by applications to support the print devices used
- Plain paper and readily available media and supplies used by printers
- Color printing devices with 256-color support and one-for-one color consistency with the user screen

- From the user device, easy (intuitive) ability to monitor printer status, change print job priority, and cancel print jobs
- Capability and quantity established by local decision
- Can be locally or network attached
- Ability to locally specify hardcopy output device-optional characteristics
- Ability to locally specify printers/plotters to meet required characteristics, such as specific paper size, resolution, speed, and color requirements

Security

- Display and input device password protection available on desktop systems through a user-configurable timeout and a hot-key sequence
- A single sign-in and password allowing user access to all authorized resources, without retyping sign-in for each resource, via automatic monthly password synchronization
- Designated information owners given the ability to establish appropriate access attributes for files, shared data sets, and directories
- Data and system security services that provide system access, data access, and access violation reports to system owners
- Security administration tools available to authorized managers to add/change/delete/monitor security privileges
- Consider operating system command-line access availability only to approved users
- Antivirus software installed on servers and PCs/workstations; capable of scanning on demand, on a schedule, and automatically on file access without conflict with other software; updated regularly with additional updates provided as needed; updates done automatically from a server; operational feature settings and configurations specifiable by local management
- Optional capability to provide total physical deletion of secured files; physical removal of file, all occurrences including archive and backups; all pointers; file shredding
- Multiple simultaneous logins available for authorized personnel
- Sender identity attached to all transmitted data files and messages

Support

- An environment supported over a stable and reliable local- and wide-area network that is common across the enterprise community
- The shared network supports PCs, workstations, and servers

- Hardware, software, and infrastructure stability and reliability with minimized downtime; optional systems able to achieve nearly 100% uptime where cost-justified
- Disaster recovery planning and procedures reviewed and fully tested at least once yearly
- All problems within the environment recorded and tracked with immediate status information available to the user
- Continuous improvement evident in relation to all activities
- Priorities in hardware maintenance management determined by user productivity
- Availability of user productivity tools that support such tasks as data transfer, file conversion, mail, and hardcopy output management
- Selection of applications and application suites determined by the local user community from a list of enterprise-endorsed common applications
- Patches and bug fixes coordinated and communicated throughout enterprise and can occur between major upgrades
- Application license sharing takes place over the network; licenses may be corporate, site, or node locked
- Ability to receive specific application support directly from the OEM or through a special agreement with another party
- Optional availability of application deinstallation, including the removal of changes made to system configuration files when installing the application

These high-level requirements are used to select technologies, and systems for the enterprise as illustrated in Figure D.1.

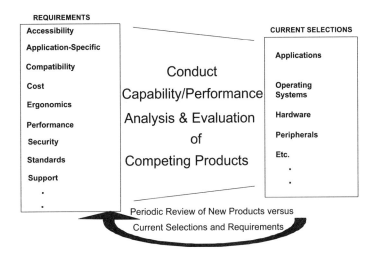

Figure D.1 Technology Selection and Evolution. Requirements must guide the selection of IT. A periodic review of new versus current technology against the same requirements will keep the IT architecture fresh.

Appendix E:
Process Classification
Framework (Generic)

Purpose

The process classification framework serves as a high-level, generic enterprise model that encourages business and other organizations to see their activities from a cross-industry, process viewpoint instead of from a narrow functional viewpoint.

All too often, organizations become bogged down by the fear of making mistakes in apples-to-oranges benchmark comparisons. Convinced that they have unique characteristics and constraints, they have difficulty understanding how to compare their processes meaningfully to different organizations.

However, experience shows that the potential of benchmarking to drive dramatic improvement often lies squarely in making out-of-the-box comparisons and a search for insights not found within typical intra-industry paradigms. How can organizations communicate effectively across industry boundaries and overcome the vocabularies that obscure the underlying commonality of their business processes?

The process classification framework supplies a generic view of business processes often found in multiple industries and sectors — manufacturing and service companies, healthcare, government, education, and others.

Additionally, many organizations now seek to understand their inner workings from a horizontal, process viewpoint rather than from a vertical, functional viewpoint. How can they, for example, differentiate the sales process from the existing sales department?

The process classification framework seeks to represent major processes and subprocesses, not functions, through its structure and vocabulary. The framework does not list all processes found within any specific organization. Likewise, not every process listed in the framework is present in every organization.

Rights and Permissions*

APQC would like to see the process classification framework receive wide distribution, discussion, and use. Therefore, APQC grants permission for copying the framework, as long as acknowledgment is made to the American Productivity & Quality Center.

1   Understand Markets and Customers
- 1.1   Determine customer needs and wants
  - 1.1.1   Conduct qualitative assessments
    - 1.1.1.1   Conduct customer interviews
    - 1.1.1.2   Conduct focus groups
  - 1.1.2   Conduct quantitative assessments
    - 1.1.2.1   Develop and implement surveys
  - 1.1.3   Predict customer purchasing behavior
- 1.2   Measure customer satisfaction
  - 1.2.1   Monitor satisfaction with products and services
  - 1.2.2   Monitor satisfaction with complaint resolution
  - 1.2.3   Monitor satisfaction with communication
- 1.3   Monitor changes in market or customer expectations
  - 1.3.1   Determine weaknesses of product/service offerings
  - 1.3.2   Identify new innovations that are meeting customers needs
  - 1.3.3   Determine customer reactions to competitive offerings

2   Develop Vision and Strategy
- 2.1   Monitor the external environment
  - 2.1.1   Analyze and understand competition
  - 2.1.2   Identify economic trends
  - 2.1.3   Identify political and regulatory issues
  - 2.1.4   Assess new technology innovations

2.1.5   Understand demographics

2.1.6   Identify social and cultural changes

2.1.7   Understand ecological concerns

2.2   Define the business concept and organizational strategy

2.2.1   Select relevant markets

2.2.2   Develop long-term vision

2.2.3   Formulate business unit strategy

2.2.4   Develop overall mission statement

2.3   Design the organizational structure and relationships between organizational units

2.4   Develop and set organizational goals

3   Design Products and Services

3.1   Develop new product/service concept and plans

3.1.1   Translate customer wants and needs into product and/or service requirements

3.1.2   Plan and deploy quality targets

3.1.3   Plan and deploy cost targets

3.1.4   Develop product life cycle and development timing targets

3.1.5   Develop and integrate leading technology into product/service concept

3.2   Design, build, and evaluate prototype products and services

3.2.1   Develop product/service specifications

3.2.2   Conduct concurrent engineering

3.2.3   Implement value engineering

3.2.4   Document design specifications

3.2.5   Develop prototypes

3.2.6   Apply for patents

3.3   Refine existing products/services

3.3.1   Develop product/service enhancements

3.3.2   Eliminate quality/reliability problems

3.3.3   Eliminate outdated products/services

3.4   Test effectiveness of new or revised products or services

3.5   Prepare for production

3.5.1   Develop and test prototype production process

3.5.2   Design and obtain necessary materials and equipment

3.5.3   Install and verify process or methodology

3.6   Manage the product/service development process

4   Market and Sell

4.1   Market products or services to relevant customer segments

4.1.1   Develop pricing strategy

4.1.2   Develop advertising strategy

6.1.1 Select and certify suppliers

6.1.2 Purchase materials and supplies

6.1.3 Acquire appropriate technology

6.2 Develop human resource skills

6.2.1 Define skill requirements

6.2.2 Identify and implement training

6.2.3 Monitor and manage skill development

6.3 Deliver service to the customer

6.3.1 Confirm specific service requirements for individual customer

6.3.2 Identify and schedule resources to meet service requirements

6.3.3 Provide the service to specific customers

6.4 Ensure quality of service

7 Invoice and Service Customers

7.1 Bill the customer

7.1.1 Develop, deliver, and maintain customer billing

7.1.2 Invoice the customer

7.1.3 Respond to billing inquiries

7.2 Provide after-sales service

7.2.1 Provide post-sales service

7.2.2 Handle warranties and claims

7.3 Respond to customer inquiries

7.3.1 Respond to information requests

7.3.2 Manage customer complaints

8 Develop and Manage Human Resources

8.1 Create and manage human resource strategies

8.1.1 Identify organizational strategic demands

8.1.2 Determine human resource costs

8.1.3 Define human resource requirements

8.1.4 Define human resource's organizational role

8.2 Cascade strategy to work level

8.2.1 Analyze, design, or redesign work

8.2.2 Define and align work outputs and metrics

8.2.3 Define work competencies

8.3 Manage deployment of personnel

8.3.1 Plan and forecast workforce requirements

8.3.2 Develop succession and career plans

8.3.3 Recruit, select and hire employees

8.3.4 Create and deploy teams

8.3.5 Relocate employees

8.3.6 Restructure and rightsize workforce

8.3.7 Manage employee retirement

9.3.1   Establish systems security strategies and levels

9.3.2   Test, evaluate, and deploy systems security and controls

9.4   Manage information storage & retrieval

9.4.1   Establish information repositories (data bases)

9.4.2   Acquire & collect information

9.4.3   Store information

9.4.4   Modify and update information

9.4.5   Enable retrieval of information

9.4.6   Delete information

9.5   Manage facilities and network operations

9.5.1   Manage centralized facilities

9.5.2   Manage distributed facilities

9.5.3   Manage network operations

9.6   Manage information services

9.6.1   Manage libraries and information centers

9.6.2   Manage business records and documents

9.7   Facilitate information sharing and communication

9.7.1   Manage external communications systems

9.7.2   Manage internal communications systems

9.7.3   Prepare and distribute publications

9.8   Evaluate and audit information quality

10 Manage Financial and Physical Resources

10.1   Manage financial resources

10.1.1   Develop budgets

10.1.2   Manage resource allocation

10.1.3   Design capital structure

10.1.4   Manage cash flow

10.1.5   Manage financial risk

10.2   Process finance and accounting transactions

10.2.1   Process accounts payable

10.2.2   Process payroll

10.2.3   Process accounts receivable, credit, and collections

10.2.4   Close the books

10.2.5   Process benefits and retiree information

10.2.6   Manage travel and entertainment expenses

10.3   Report information

10.3.1   Provide external financial information

10.3.2   Provide internal financial information

10.4   Conduct internal audits

10.5   Manage the tax function

10.5.1   Ensure tax compliance

10.5.2   Plan tax strategy

Appendix F: Information Resources Management

Introduction

Information resources management is a pivotal support enabler for integrated and virtual enterprise. This section discusses methods to ensure that information is exploitable for the best interest of the enterprise. The enterprise's data management view is discussed first, followed by a discussion of the information technology (IT) view, which realizes the exploitation of enterprise information.

This section does not recommend any specific IT systems, e.g., ERP, MRP, PDM, etc. Acknowledging there is always a requirement for these IT systems, this discussion concentrates on COTS technology that can provide the integration of systems from an enterprise perspective. When implementing integration software, there is no such thing as a one-size-fits-all solution. However, there is some COTS software (middleware, described later in this section) that fits most cases. This type of reusable integration technology should be implemented where possible. Development of software for point-to-point integration should be avoided where possible.

Data Management View

The implementation of data management is different for various companies depending on their business. The vision and strategies for a physically distributed manufacturing consortium that must act as a single, virtual enterprise are different from those for a bank or product distribution company.

Figure F.1 illustrates that data is managed, organized, and then exploited for the enterprise. An understanding of the data to be managed is derived from the processes utilized within the enterprise life cycle to develop, deliver, and support products and services. In the same tone, the management, organization, and exploitation methods developed from the data management strategies are implemented with the enterprise processes and users' requirements in mind. The data management processes must coexist with and enable the other processes utilized within the enterprise. It is necessary to understand and capture the relationships among the different data elements that are shared or joined if a common understanding of the resultant information is required.

Data (information) management is the major component of the information ecosystem. An information ecosystem, as defined by W. H. Inmon in his book, *Corporate Information Factory,* "is a system with different components, each serving a community directly while working in concert with other components to produce a cohesive, balanced information environment. Like nature's ecosystem, an information ecosystem must be adaptable, changing as the inhabitants and participants within its aegis change."

Data Organization

In order to exploit enterprise data, that is, create information views on demand, it is necessary to capture some knowledge of the data types, definitions, and structures, as well as the data content itself. This data about the data is called metadata. Figure F.2 illustrates that data is widely distributed within an enterprise. When data customers require information for a given task, they may have to look in multiple places for various elements of the data. When metadata is available to the client, the shopping experience is made much easier.

Some of the items described by the metadata include security requirements to access the data, where the data is stored, how the data is stored, the format of the data, and a description of the data (usually from the data dictionary). By using the proper tools, a query can be generated that uses metadata about the enterprise's various databases to obtain data from multiple sources and join them into a single information view. An extended shopping trip to many stores becomes one-stop shopping.

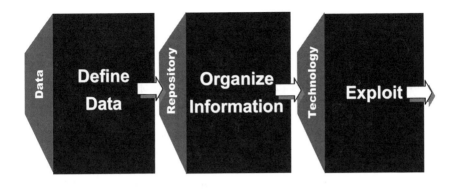

Figure F.1   Data Management View. This figure illustrates that the data to be managed must be recognized and organized before it can be exploited.

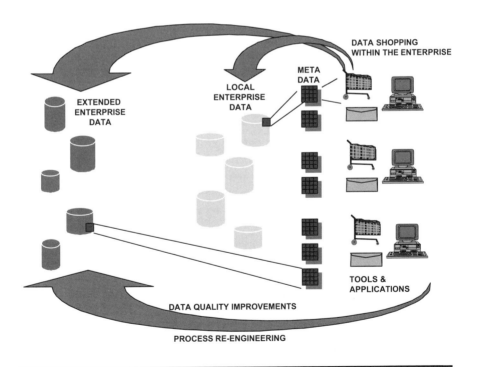

Figure F.2   Distributed Data within the Enterprise.

Several data integration technologies can be brought to bear at this point. The COTS technologies discussed here all support data modeling, the organization of data, and metadata. These technologies are discussed in the following categories: point-to-point solutions, data warehouses, data marts, operational data stores, and virtual data integration. These categories have one thing in common. They all use middleware to accomplish data integration.

The Gartner Group defines middleware as "that breed of software residing between the user's application and operating systems, concealing the complexities of network protocols, database dialects, and operating system flavors as data requests are interpreted and routed through an organization." All of these technologies/methods, with the exception of point-to-point solutions, utilize off-the-shelf middleware tools, and the vendors have metadata capture tools that can be employed with the middle ware. Point-to-point solutions may contain these types of tools, but caution is advised.

Point-to-point solutions utilize application programming interface software, such as C++ and Visual Basic, to create direct, individual interfaces between required data contained within two or more information systems. The concern with this method is that each interface is usually created specifically for a certain report or need and is generally not rationalized within the context of reuse. Stated differently, point-to-point solutions are data translations; they are not a logical organization of data designed for multiple and repeated use. Point-to-point solutions typically result in a spiderweb of interfaces. Multiple types of interfaces among the various applications' physical data stores must all be managed. The difficulty and cost of maintaining any magnitude of specific interfaces quickly become detrimental to the enterprise.

A data warehouse (DW) is a data organization technique that primarily builds a group of subject areas derived from the enterprise data model. Some examples of subject areas are marketing, sales, engineering, and manufacturing. The information in these subject areas is used in the enterprise's decision-making processes to provide knowledge-based solutions to enterprise needs.

Accessible data in a DW is normally 24 hours to 2 years old (sometimes older). Data extraction, cleansing, and transformation tools are used to move the data from local databases into the DW. Until recently, batch-mode processing was normally used to store data, and it was accomplished during user off-hours. Large data stores (i.e., massive data storage devices) are required to house the data.

Application programming interfaces (APIs) are utilized to allow application developers to talk to the data stores. An application development tool (which may be the same as the API) is then used to create the interface to the user. This type of integration technology is widely used for data mining — a technique for defining trends and potential customer needs.

Recently the DW has been recognized as a place to store information that needs to be shared with the extended enterprise. Access to the DW allows vendors and subcontractors to directly view vital information, which enhances accuracy and agility in the supply chain processes.

Data marts are primarily the same as data warehouses except they generally contain information about one subject area and are more commonly used to integrate information in concert with a data model that may be later integrated with an enterprise model. The same type of software is used to extract data from multiple application data stores; and a data dictionary and metadata capture mechanism must be in place. This allows for reuse of the data elements within the enterprise and for expansion.

Operational data stores (ODS) have much in common with data warehouses and data marts. They utilize some of the same technology, but the primary difference is that an ODS contains more volatile data. An ODS is treated more like a transactional system. A transactional system is described as a system used primarily for a functional operation such as financial, CAD, logistics, and project management. The data contained within an ODS is normally one minute to one year old. An ODS may also be used on a limited basis as a transactional system.

A data warehouse, mart, or operational store provides each API with the ability to do one-stop shopping by using metadata about the source databases to create a physically consolidated database. The next evolution of data organization also creates a consolidated database for the APIs, but this database is virtual, not physical. The virtual data integration approach uses the notion of data models and data maps to create a layer of middleware that is perceived by the APIs as a consolidated database, but in reality allows the data to physically reside in multiple native database stores. Where needed for performance, memory caches may be added to the middleware for frequently accessed data; but for the most part, the need to rehost the data physically (as the data warehouse approach does) is avoided.

Virtual data integration uses an *N*-tier (usually a minimum of 5 tiers) approach to the integration and distribution of data. The intent is to allow uncoupling at each of the tiers to isolate the effects of modification. The multilayered approach makes it much easier to insert newer or different tools. Figure F.3 illustrates a five-tier approach:

Tier 1 — Data extraction
Tier 2 — Integration and transformation
Tier 3 — API development
Tier 4 — Utilization of application development tools
Tier 5 — Client's view of the information

Figure F.3 also illustrates that data management is integral to the transformation operation.

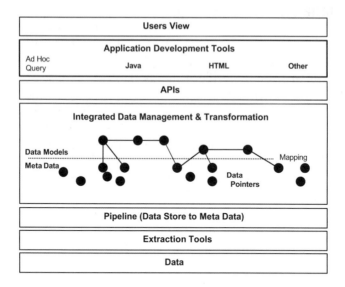

Figure F.3 *N*-Tiered Integrated Data Management. The *N*-tiers approach allows the decoupling at the data stores, gateways, integrated management and transformation, API, and application development tools level.

The virtual data integration approach creates a virtual database between third-party application development and API software and third-party query and data extraction software. Data models are created to describe the data objects and data relationships (i.e., rules) needed by the client views. Application and API layers request information for the client in logical form (model form). The integration and transformation layer uses metadata and a map of the physical data stores to create physical queries of the native database. After the data is physically extracted from its source database(s), the virtual database again uses the metadata to join the various pieces of data into information in the model form. The information is then provided to the client back through the API and application layers.

Changes in the organization of the physical data now ripple only as far as the virtual database. The metadata and maps may need to be adjusted in the middleware, but the models are unchanged. From the other side of the virtual database, the API, application, and client layers of information never sensed a change.

Virtual data integration is now becoming a reality and has advantages over the other technologies and methods. However, it must also be remembered that the amount of data to be accessed also has an impact on which solution is best.

Data Management Planning

Data management is the definition, implementation, and maintenance of consistent global data standards across the entire enterprise, focused on enabling the implementation of shared information systems and processes. Its benefits are improved accuracy in communication, reduced lead times, improved decision-making, managed configuration of systems, and consistent implementation across IT providers. Global data standards are accomplished by developing standard names and definitions, standard permitted values, and standard business rule definitions.

Figure F.4 illustrates a data management planning process that moves from a strategic position to an operational position. The elements illustrated allow for an overall plan, a development cycle, change management, a repository for data models and the data dictionary, and a release process for managing new and/or required change. Several tools allow these to be captured in metadata catalogs. One strategy might allow the user some leeway in the definition of new data merges, while having the majority of the data under administrative or change control.

Data Exploitation

Data exploitation is data that is displayed and then used within the enterprise. A network architecture, IT systems, and applications are required to produce the views for the enterprise business, engineering,

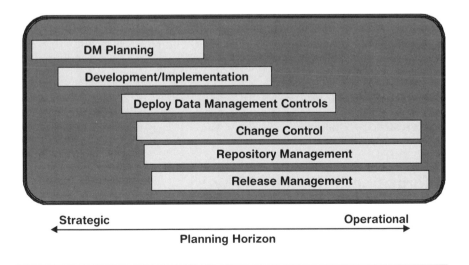

Figure F.4   Data Management Planning and Implementation.

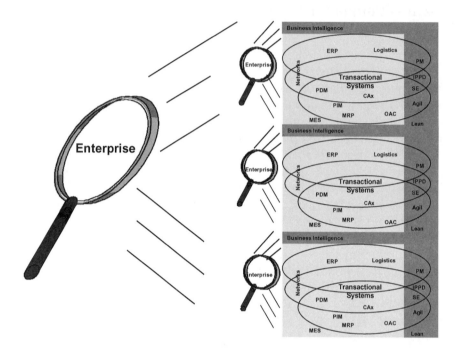

Figure F.5   Data Exploitation Views. Common COTS software technology can have a positive effect on creating the virtual enterprise.

manufacturing, delivery, and support and dismantling operations and processes. This is the enterprise life cycle. Figure F.5 illustrates that one enterprise view in most cases includes someone else's enterprise view. Creating these views requires a flexible, agile IT architecture, utilizing as much common COTS software as possible. This allows multiple enterprises to become part of the virtual enterprise at the lowest cost and greatest productivity.

Information Technology View

The information technology (IT) view of the enterprise describes the technology enablers for operating the enterprise. The IT view is referred to as an enterprise-wide information technology infrastructure view, or just information technology infrastructure view (ITIV) for short. The ITIV is the enabling infrastructure for the evolution of the enterprise information architectures. The primary objective of the ITIV is to achieve interoperability within the enterprise. The architecture will define a logical structure able to give any enterprise activity appropriate access to required information.

Definition of an ITIV

The ITIV is an enterprise-wide communications system for voice, data, and video that extends to all enterprise sites, including those of its suppliers. The enterprise network services the needs of all parts of the enterprise and will provide interfaces to the enterprise networks to the extended enterprise. Figure F.6 depicts an IT functional view of the enterprise and a relationship of the business, information, and technology components.

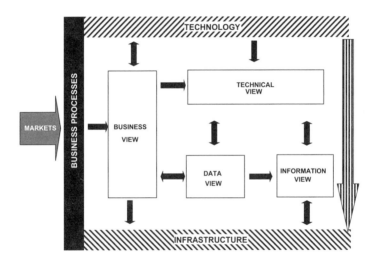

Figure F.6   Top-Level IT View of the Enterprise.

ITIV Planning

Each enterprise must establish an ITIV. This will be based on aligning requirements derived from the enterprise processes and strategies as they are viewed at the implementation level. The ITIV provides a set of guidelines for centralized and decentralized network and systems implementation efforts that specify a target for topologies, technologies, and standards. The principal features of the architecture include identified points of technical stability that maximize investments, prevent premature obsolescence, and minimize disruption to users. The ITIV also features standards that support long-term stability by promoting technical convergence. These standards will maximize interoperability while minimizing management complexity. Standards also simplify and reduce incompatibilities and complexities.

The ITIV is not complete without considering the current and future states of the enterprise. Unfortunately, this is often overlooked, at least in the early stages. Information systems (IS) teams are typically eager to jump into the technology arena without comprehending business drivers. This results in poor focus and lack of management support. These projects never develop to their full potential.

Migration to Open Systems

An important aspect of the best-practice ITIV is that the architecture promotes the transition to open systems information technology. The enterprise network must support the use of open systems protocols and adhere itself to the principles of open systems architecture. This means that the enterprise network must

- Clearly support business objectives
- Use information technology products, both hardware and software, that are interchangeable and that interoperate within and across enterprises
- Support transport and portability of both applications and data
- Be modular, extensible, scalable, and easily integrated
- Be based on standards that are well defined by public, consensus-based, vendor-neutral specifications

Business Drivers for the ITIV

The adoption of the ITIV will bring significant business benefits in easier access to information; greater cross-workgroup and cross-organization cooperation and synergy; faster cycle time in all business processes; and a simpler, easier-to-manage, and less costly infrastructure.

Meeting Business Goals

The ITIV is like a highway system. Without a good highway system, it is almost impossible for an economy to grow and be efficient since materials and finished goods can't get from one place to another efficiently. For the enterprise, the ITIV is crucial to meeting time-to-market goals and to implementing concurrent engineering practices. Timely access to information is a prerequisite to all efforts to increase the enterprise's operational effectiveness and engineer business processes.

Information Systems (IS) and Technology Goals

As an example, a modern network is essential to progress in the use of information technology in the enterprise. All new application systems make heavy use of the network for real-time data interchange. Most new application development is being done in the Web-based client–server model in order to exploit cost-effective low-end systems. Throughout the enterprise, IS organizations should be planning to put fewer and fewer applications on centralized mainframes and target new applications to distributed approaches. The enterprise may need an updated architecture if this transition to distributed computing is going to succeed.

Applications will make greater use of visual information in the form of imaging, including 3D CAD and video. These applications will increase the capacity requirements on the network by two or three orders of magnitude. The ITIV must be able to scale gracefully when new application technologies are implemented.

Overview of the ITIV

The ITIV may be viewed as three principal subarchitectures:

- The physical view: This portion of the architecture primarily addresses connectivity
- The logical view: This portion of the architecture primarily addresses transport interoperability
- The network management view: This portion of the architecture primarily addresses manageability

In each of these views, coping with diversity and change is the key problem to be solved. Organizations may find themselves deploying a large variety of systems throughout the enterprise. Meanwhile, new and improved technologies are being brought to market steadily. As the number of technologies increases, so do management complexity and overall cost. This ITIV attempts to balance support for a diverse and changing set of technologies by establishing a management framework that is simple and cost-effective.

An ITIV Supports Centralized and Decentralized Management

The view balances the needs of individual sites with the needs of the enterprise. It recognizes that the enterprise systems and networks span multiple administrative and management domains and is a shared resource managed in a shared, cooperative manner.

Assignment of administrative and management responsibilities to particular organizations is always changing.

ITIV and Data/Information Integration

A robust ITIV, developed in unison with the enterprise information architectures, creates an environment where necessary data flows freely — yet securely — to all units of the enterprise. Figure F.7 depicts what we'll call the integrated data view of the enterprise. This is a high-level representation of some of the typical components and data flows that one might expect to encounter in a TIE. While perhaps not obvious in this diagram, the ITIV underlies the entire view. This can often be one of the dilemmas in the IT world, not being readily apparent yet vitally important. While we don't see the ITIV called out in this diagram, everything depends on its presence.

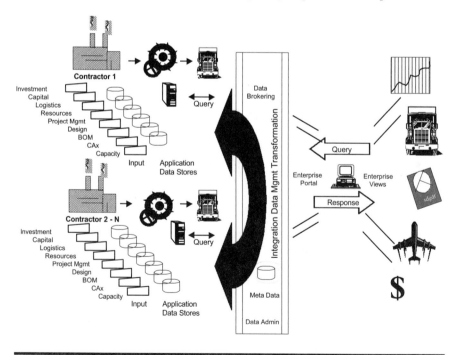

Figure F.7   Integrated Data View for Enterprise. This is a high-level representation of typical components and data flows in a virtual enterprise.

In this illustration, the view of the enterprise resides on the right, with various remote sites, contractors, suppliers, etc., on the left. As needs are identified — either by management or by field inputs — queries are submitted and responses issued. If there is a request for inventory status, for example, it is routed to the appropriate supplier, warehouse, or whatever (where more routing or transformation may occur). The return response is once again routed where it is transformed and routed back to the requestor. All of this, of course, is delivered and communicated across the IT infrastructure, which is encompassed within the ITIV. Appendix E provides a summary list illustrating some requirements that should be questioned when evaluating technology or products for an enterprise application, system, or technical solution.

ITIV Summary

An ITIV will plot a course toward a simplified and rational enterprise with interoperable communications throughout the enterprise. It supports a diverse installed base and provides for the integration of new technologies and systems, as they become important.

The ITIV view proposes a greater degree of centralization in provisioning and management. A core will have responsibility for all campus level, metro-area, and wide-area communication. It will enforce standards for protocols and distributed computing services and will implement enterprise-wide management that will be shared by different sites.

The view will scale to meet expected demands over the next five years through such strategies as, micro-segmentation of LANs, the use of dedicated 802.3 interfaces, and the use of ATM cell switching, for example.

The ITIV offers the following efficiency opportunities:

■ Greater use of virtual public services, reducing capital requirements and exploiting shared facilities whenever there is a business advantage
■ Consolidation of parallel group-level networks onto a single enterprise backbone and the sharing of wide-area, metro-, and campus-level networks by all enterprise systems and organizations
■ Modular and selective application of redundancy where requirements dictate
■ Standardization on single, strategic vendors for simplifying management, support, and servicing, and upgrades
■ Greater centralization of campus, metro- and wide-area network management and administration, promoting economies of scale and less duplication of effort, concurrent and collaborative environments

Appendix G: Enterprise Assessment

An enterprise assessment establishes a baseline that allows leadership to identify improvement projects with the most leverage and it forms a reference point for measuring progress.

Overview

Conducting assessments is an everyday occurrence in most businesses. What distinguishes one assessment from another is their individual purpose and scope, which, in turn, affect the level of detail of the data collected and the effort required. A critical step in any change process is to clearly understand and document the current state. The need to define the current state is required when assessing an entity as large and complex as an enterprise. A compelling vision of the future may already be in place. But in order to plan and embark upon a journey to achieve the vision, the enterprise must know from where it is beginning and exactly what will be changed. Progress can then be monitored to provide feedback on the success of improvement efforts or to identify the need for midcourse corrections.

Enterprise assessment is a process that interrogates all processes used within an organization and that gathers data. The importance of knowledge-based decisions supported by facts and data is underscored by the fact that just about everyone in any enterprise has an opinion of how things are and what should be done next. The problem is that rarely does one person have all the facts, and for those that one does have, the interpretation may not be consistent with the interpretations of others. Therefore, an assessment is used to establish a baseline that all parties must agree upon before additional resources are applied to the deployment of improvement initiatives.

One approach to guiding an enterprise assessment is through use of the enterprise process framework identified in the section on integrated product and process development in Chapter 5. This model is similar to the Process Classification Framework developed by the American Productivity & Quality Center that is listed in Appendix E of this book. Both models supply a generic view of business processes often found in multiple industries and sectors — manufacturing and service companies, healthcare, government, education, and others. Both seek to represent major processes and subprocesses, not functions, through its structure and vocabulary. It should be noted that neither lists all processes found within any specific organization. Likewise, not every process listed in the framework is present in every organization. The models serve as high-level, generic enterprise models that encourage business and other organizations to see their activities from a cross-industry, process-focused viewpoint instead of from a narrow functional one.

The time needed to conduct an assessment is highly dependent on an organization's size, complexity, geographic distribution, and ability to allocate resources to the effort. The assessment activity itself is intense and requires access to people and data at all levels of the organization. The more quickly an assessment can be completed, the better, because it is the resultant information that stimulates dialog, consensus, plans, action, and ultimately, improvement.

An enterprise assessment typically consists of interviews, visits to work areas, observations of work practices, reviews of process descriptions, and reviews of appropriate metrics and other indicators/predictors. While an assessment can be completed by an external agency, the depth of understanding and richness of the data is enhanced when enterprise personnel are included as integral members of the assessment team. Facilitated by an external agency and supported with internal resources, enterprise self-assessment results can maintain a level of objectivity and credibility that withstands organizational scrutiny.

Knowledge gained from an analysis and evaluation of the data gathered during the enterprise assessment allows the enterprise leadership to identify priorities, resources, and plans for launching improvement initiatives.

Table G.I lists some major processes addressed by an enterprise assessment. Survey instruments, including questionnaires and interview questions, are structured to gather data and provide information in accordance with the categories listed in the enterprise process framework.

Assessment Tools and Techniques

The enterprise assessment process uses data gathering, analysis, and display tools to provide information that allows leadership to prioritize improvement initiatives and commit resources to projects that will provide the largest returns and most leverage across the enterprise.

A sound, structured problem-solving process begins with a clear definition of the problem, continues with gathering data to accurately describe the current state, then proceeds through an analysis and evaluation phase before solutions are contemplated. The enterprise assessment is focused on the determination of the current state and the tools used usually include data-gathering tools, flowcharts, Pareto charts, time plots, frequency plots (histograms), and control charts.

Even before any tools are used, it is important to establish operational definitions, definitions that describe what will be measured and how it will be measured. This helps overcome the imprecision that is a part of daily conversations and ensures repeatability of measurements regardless of who performs the measurement.

Tools used for data gathering include prepared interview questions, computer queries, questionnaires, checksheets (or checklists), and work-flow diagrams. Interview questions, questionnaires, and checklists must be self-explanatory and specific to a process being investigated. Workflow diagrams depict the movement of products, material, people, documentation, or information and are sometimes called spaghetti charts. Needless to say, good data is essential for subsequent tools to be of value.

Flowcharts are used to map processes. The level of detail and structure of flowcharts vary based upon need. A high-level flowchart outlines the major steps in a process and is used when an overview is sufficient. If the next level of substeps is added under each major step, then a top-down flowchart is being created. Adding responsible organizations or functions to a flowchart results in a process map.

Pareto charts, time plots, frequency plots, and control charts are used for looking at data relationships. As a part of the assessment process, these tools bring information to light, allow analysis and evaluation to be performed, and are the next logical step in determining what really needs to be solved. These types of charts are effective in telling the story because they are based on data. Disagreements can be resolved by reviewing the

Table G.1 Enterprise Assessment Structure Based on Process Framework

Strategic Processes	Core Processes	Enabler Processes
Executive leadership	**Customer acquisition**	• Human resources management
• Leadership — vision, mission, values, expectations	• Product awareness	• Information resources management
	• Order-taking	• Financial and physical resources management
• Strategic direction — customers, business processes, people, shareholders		• Environment policy management
		• External relationships management
• Deployment and execution — capability, cultural change, growth	**Product realization**	• Improvement and change management
	• Product creation	
• Results — customer satisfaction, competitive advantage, teamwork, shareholder value	• Product delivery	
	Product and customer support	
Business development	• Feedback and support	
• Markets and customers	• Product dismantling	
• Supply/demand chain management		
• Competitive analysis		
• Corporate alignment		
• Research and development		
• Technology management		
• Product program launch		
• Portfolio management		

data, the source of the data, or the completeness of the data. The important point is that data speaks for itself.

The output of the enterprise assessment is a report that clearly and succinctly portrays the current state of the enterprise. Combined with comparison to the declared vision, it can identify the nature and magnitude of the gap between the vision and the current state of the enterprise. This is the information leadership needs to begin the process of prioritizing the steps (projects) that must be initiated to eliminate the gap and move the enterprise to a higher level of competitive performance.

Figure G.1 shows the enterprise assessment process and examples of some of the types of tools utilized. Preparation includes awareness briefings and training for members of the assessment team and those closely associated with the assessment effort and results. The enterprise assessment is complete when consensus has been reached on the description of the current state. The gap between the current state and the vision can be determined. It is then possible for leadership to prioritize improvement opportunities across the enterprise and sponsor those improvement initiatives that provide the largest benefit and leverage for the resources allocated.

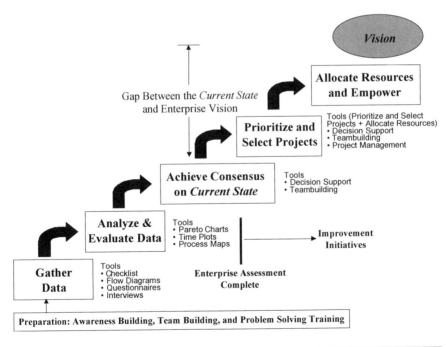

Figure G.1 Enterprise Assessment Process. Clearly defining and understanding the current state are essential in order to sponsor those improvement initiatives that optimize progress toward the enterprise vision.

Appendix H:
Federal Enterprise
Architecture Framework

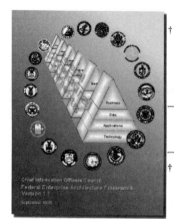

Federal Enterprise Architecture Framework

Version 1.1
September 1999

The undersigned chairs do hereby endorse this Federal Enterprise Architecture Framework and consider it to be a road map for the Federal Government in achieving better alignment of technology solutions with business mission needs.

James Flyzik, Chief Information Officer,
Department of the Treasury
Vice-Chair, CIO Council

Marvin Langston, Deputy CIO,
Department of Defense
Co-Chair, Emerging Information Technology
and Interoperability Committee

Lee Holcomb, CIO, National Aeronautics
and Space Administration
Co-Chair, Emerging Information Technology
and Interoperability Committee

Rob Thomas II, A/Director,
Technology and Architecture Group,
Chief Architect,
U.S. Customs Service
Co-Chair, Architecture Working Group

Michael A. Tiemann, Director,
Architecture and Standards Division,
Chief Architect,
Department of Energy
Co-Chair, Architecture Working Group

Credits

The members of the Federal Architecture Framework Subgroup are gratefully acknowledged for their contributions to the information presented in this document. The Subgroup members are identified below.

Name	Title	Agency
George Brundage	Architecture*Plus* PM	General Services Administration (GSA)
Crystal Bush	Program Analyst	Department of Transportation (DOT)
William Bush, Jr.	Systems Analyst	Department of Education (ED)
Martha Cain	Program Analyst	GSA
Vicki Cordes	Computer Specialist	Department of Veterans Affairs (VA)
Manny DeVera	Systems Acquisition Specialist	GSA
Ira Grossman	Systems Engineer	National Oceanic Atmospheric Administration (NOAA)
Adele Graham	Information Management Specialist	Department of Defense (DOD)
Terry Hagle	Sr. Policy Analyst	DOD
Gonza L. Kirksey	Program Manager	GSA
Timothy Mallon	Enterprise Information Analyst	Environmental Protection Agency (EPA)
Eric Mandel	Data Acquisition Manager	NOAA
Anne Mangiafico	Enterprise Information Analyst	EPA
Asghar Noor	Chief Architect	Department of the Treasury (TREAS)
Greg Pace	Dep. Dir., Office of Systems Planning	Social Security Administration (SSA)
Alan Proctor	Chief Information Officer	Federal Trade Commission (FTC)
David Prompovitch	Project Manager	DOT
Leslie Roberts	Manager, IT Arch. & Strategic Planning	Department of the Interior (DOI)
Karen Stewart	Chief Architect	SSA
Michael A. Tiemann	Dir. Arch. & Stnds Div., Chief Architect	Department of Energy (DOE)
Rob C. Thomas	Chief Architect	U.S. Customs Service
Francine Yoder	Chief Architect	EPA

The Subgroup acknowledges the work of the various groups that provided valuable recommendations and information and contributed to this document.

Panel of Experts	Groups
Dr. Steven Spewak Enterprise Architects, Inc. John Zachman ZIFA Institute and Pinnacle Group	Members of the Interoperability Committee of the CIO Council Members of the IT Resources Board (ITRB) Members of the Architecture*Plus* Community Various industry groups

†

Support Contractors			
Sue Farrand, DynCorp Kelly Flynn, DynCorp	Connie German, DynCorp Drury Norris, DynCorp	Tom Midlam, DynCorp Maura Rehling, DynCorp	Pat G. Simmons, DynCorp Mary White, DynCorp

Special recognition is extended to Francine Yoder and George Brundage for their work as Chairpersons of the Federal Architecture Framework Subgroup and to Michael Tiemann for his work as the Chairperson of the Federal Agency Information Architecture Working Group.

Contents

Introduction

Background

Executive Order 13011, *Federal Information Technology*, established the Chief Information Officers (CIO) Council as the principal interAgency forum for improving practices in the design, modernization, use, sharing, and performance of Agency information resources.

The CIO Council began developing the Federal Enterprise Architecture Framework in April†1998. The*CIO Council Strategic Plan*, dated January 1998, guided by priorities of the Clinger-Cohen Act of 1996, directed the development and maintenance of a Federal Enterprise Architecture to maximize the benefits of information technology (IT) within the Government. According to this Strategic Plan, architectures for selected high priority, cross-Agency business lines or segments will be developed to populate the Federal Enterprise Architecture. The Framework provides a sustainable mechanism for identifying, developing, and documenting architecture descriptions of high priority areas built on common business areas and designs that cross organizational boundaries.

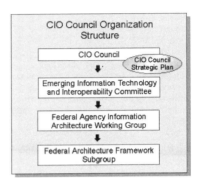

The Federal Enterprise Architecture Framework provides an organized structure and a collection of common terms by which Federal segments can integrate their respective architectures into the Federal Enterprise Architecture.

The CIO Council developed the Framework, which is nonrestrictive and easily adaptable to all Federal Agencies especially those with existing architectures. The CIO Council and its related working groups consist of representatives from many Agencies, whose contributions include protecting the interests of architecture efforts within their organizations and recognizing the need for a Governmentwide approach.

What elements comprise the Federal Enterprise?

The Federal Enterprise includes organizations of the Federal Government and all partners. Federal organizations refers to Tier 1-Large Major Federal Departmental Systems, Tier 2-Departmental Subagency and Bureau Systems, and Tier 3-All Other Federal Agency Systems.

The focus of the Federal Enterprise Architecture is limited to the common Federal architecture issues, which benefit Federal organizations and the public.

At the onset, the CIO Council agreed to use the widely accepted National Institute of Standards and Technology (NIST) model[1] (exhibit†1) and expand on this foundation to meet the organizational and management needs of a Federal Enterprise Architecture. The NIST model has been promoted within the Federal Government as a management tool that illustrates the interrelationship of enterprise business, information, and technology environments. The five-layered model allows for organizing, planning, and building an integrated set of information and information technology architectures. The five layers are defined separately but are interrelated and interwoven.

The CIO Council has adopted architecture layers similar to the NIST model for the Federal Enterprise Architecture Framework with a slightly different concept of the Federal Enterprise that reflects recent IT advancements.

Exhibit 1, NIST Enterprise Architecture Model

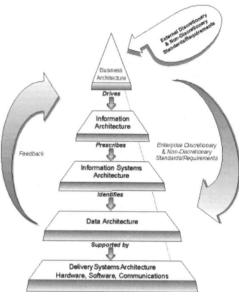

---

1 †NIST Special Publication 500-167, Information Management Directions:† The Integration Challenge.† September 1989.

The Federal Enterprise Architecture is a strategic information asset base that defines the business, information necessary to operate the business, technologies necessary to support the business operations, and transitional processes for implementing new technologies in response to the changing needs of the business.

The Federal Enterprise Architecture Framework is a conceptual model that begins to define a documented and coordinated structure for cross-cutting businesses and design developments in the Government. Collaboration among the Agencies with a vested interest in a Federal segment will result in increased efficiency and economies of scale. Agencies should use the Framework to describe segments of their architectures.

Purpose

The Federal Enterprise Architecture Framework promotes shared development for common Federal processes, interoperability, and sharing of information among Federal Agencies and other Governmental entities.

Why develop a Federal Enterprise Architecture Framework?

A Federalwide collaboration tool is needed to collect common architecture information and build a repository for storing this information. A Federal Enterprise Architecture Framework is such a tool and repository. The Framework allows the Federal Government to accomplish the following.

- ❑ Organize Federal information on a Federalwide scale
- ❑ Promote information sharing among Federal organizations
- ❑ Help Federal organizations develop their architectures
- ❑ Help Federal organizations quickly develop their IT investment processes
- ❑ Serve customer needs better, faster, and cost effectively

---

As mandated in the Clinger-Cohen Act of 1996, Federal Agencies must develop and maintain an enterprise IT architecture. Increasingly, Federal Agencies are finding that architecture development is tied to capital IT investment planning processes. This development process is, even at an Agency level, a large, complex, resource-intensive effort. By collaborating on cross-cutting activities, Federal Agencies can share staff efforts and products, thereby leveraging budget resources and lessening burdens. Collaboration can also encourage development of interoperability standards, which in turn, promote Federalwide information sharing and common capabilities. A better understanding of common Federal processes, information, and other areas where economies of scale might be applied can also evolve through collaboration.

The Federal Enterprise Architecture Framework is recommended for use in the following efforts.

- ❑ Federal Governmentwide efforts
- ❑ Multi-Federal Agency (i.e., two or more Agencies) efforts
- ❑ Whenever Federal business areas and substantial Federal investments are involved with international, State, or local governments

The goal of the CIO Council is to develop a framework to prepare an enterprise architecture description (i.e., the architecture). The Framework consists of various approaches, models, and definitions for communicating the overall organization and relationships of architecture components required for developing and maintaining a Federal Enterprise Architecture. The Framework must be flexible to allow for new activities and focus on common Federal Enterprise Architecture activities, address the realities of the Federal workplace, and provide immediate successes.

This document does not define the Federal Enterprise Architecture content; rather, it defines an organizational framework and architecture activities place-holder for future population of Federal Enterprise Architecture information.

The value of the Federal Enterprise Architecture Framework is that it provides a mechanism for linking Agency Federal Architecture activities, and promotes the development of quick successes within an overall Federal Architecture plan. This link allows Agencies to work their architecture issues within the broader context of the Federal Enterprise Architecture to reap the benefits of resource sharing and interoperability. Additionally, by allowing for quick successes, the model addresses real-world business needs of initiatives that provide strategic value.

What is the value of a Federal Enterprise Architecture Framework?

- ❑ Promote Federal *interoperability*
- ❑ Promote Agency *resource sharing*
- ❑ Provide potential for Federal and Agency *reduced costs*
- ❑ Improve ability to *share information*
- ❑ Support Federal and Agency *capital IT investment planning*

Approach

In developing the Federal Enterprise Architecture Framework, the CIO Council evaluated three approaches.

❑ **Conventional Approach** - Requires a substantial initial investment in time and dollars. First, a framework must be developed that shows how to prepare an architecture description. Second, the current baseline must be described. Finally, a target architecture must be described. Only after these activities are completed, implementing needed architecture changes through design, development, and acquisition of systems can begin. Although this approach appears to be sound, it may result in "paralysis by analysis," because of the complexity of the Federal effort.

❑ **Segment Approach** - Promotes the incremental development of architecture segments within a structured enterprise architecture framework. This approach focuses on major business areas (e.g., grants or common financial systems) and is more likely to succeed because the effort is limited to common functions or specific enterprises.

❑ **Status Quo Approach** - Represents business as usual resulting in continued failure to share information and cope with the rapidly changing environment. This approach would result in business rework, decreased productivity, and lost and missed opportunities, as well as failure to comply with Clinger-Cohen Act requirements.

Today, many initiatives and interAgency efforts are underway for implementing Agency architectures. Agency initiatives are necessary to support Federal business needs and should not be delayed pending the development of current and target Federal Architectures. The Federal Enterprise Architecture effort should not impede individual Agency architecture efforts.

To mitigate the risk of overreaching with minimal returns, curtail startup costs for a conventional architecture, and realize returns quickly, the CIO Council selected the segment approach.

A conventional architecture methodology would probably cease in-progress architecture initiatives to develop Federalwide current and target architectures. Obviously, this paradigm is unrealistic and does not meet Government business needs. The solution is a framework that supports immediate response to urgent Agency business needs. The Federal Enterprise Architecture Framework allows critical parts of the overall Federal Enterprise, called architectural segments, to be developed individually, while integrating these segments into the larger Enterprise Architecture. In May 1999, the CIO Council drafted a process for identifying and approving Federal segments. The CIO Council proposed a form or petition for designating a Federal information architecture segment. The form is provided as appendix A, Petition to be Designated a Federal Information Architecture Segment. For more information on identifying and approving Federal segments, visit the Architecture*Plus* web site (refer to appendix D, References).

Framework Components

In designing the Framework, the CIO†Council identified eight components necessary for developing and maintaining the Federal Enterprise Architecture, then drilled down to a further granularity of detail. The flow and detail of the Framework are discussed in the Federal Enterprise Architecture Framework section of this document. The following is a brief overview of the eight Framework components.

Architecture Drivers - Represent two types of external stimuli or change agents for the enterprise architecture: business and design. The business drivers could be new legislation, new administration initiatives, budget enhancements for accelerated focus areas, and market forces. Design drivers include new and enhanced software and hardware and their combinations with a variety of deployment approaches.

Strategic Direction - Guides the development of the target architecture and consists of a vision, principles, and goals and objectives.

Current Architecture - Defines the "as is" enterprise architecture and consists of two parts: current business and design architectures (i.e., data, applications, and technology). This is a representation of current capabilities and technologies and is expanded as additional segments are defined.

Target Architecture - Defines the "to-be-built" enterprise architecture and consists of two parts: target business and design architectures (i.e., data, applications, and technology). This represents the future capabilities and technologies resulting from design enhancements to support changing business needs.

Transitional Processes - Support the migration from the current to the target architecture. Critical transition processes for the Federal Enterprise include capital IT investment planning, migration planning, configuration management, and engineering change control.

Architectural Segments - Consist of focused architecture efforts on major cross-cutting business areas, such as common administrative systems; program areas, such as trade and grants; or small purchases via electronic commerce. They represent a portion (segment) of the overall enterprise architecture. A segment is considered to be an enterprise within the total Federal Enterprise.

Architectural Models - Define the business and design models that comprise the segments of the enterprise description.

Standards - Refer to all standards (some of which may be mandatory), guidelines, and best practices.

Federal Enterprise Architecture Vision and Principles

The Federal Enterprise Architecture vision and principles are based upon recent laws that address the importance of getting results, obtaining maximum return-on-investment and cost efficiency of operations, providing quality information and technology, protecting privacy, maintaining secure information, and providing service to the public.

Vision

The Federal Enterprise Architecture vision, adopted by the CIO Council, identifies *what* must be done to serve the strategic needs and direction of the Federal Government.

The Federal CIO Council seeks to develop, maintain, and facilitate the implementation of the top-level enterprise architecture for the Federal Enterprise. This architecture will serve as a reference point to facilitate the efficient and effective coordination of common business processes, information flows, systems, and investments among Federal Agencies. In time, Government business processes and systems will operate seamlessly in an enterprise architecture that provides models and standards that identify and define the information services used throughout the Government.

Principles

The Federal Enterprise Architecture principles adopted by the CIO Council govern and represent the criteria against which all potential investment and architectural decisions are weighed.

1. **Standards** *Establish Federal interoperability standards.*

Rationale: The Federal Government has not achieved data, applications, and technology interoperability. Connectivity is often the last requirement addressed. It is difficult to control lifecycle costs and schedules and improve performance, take advantage of commercial items and technology, and maintain and evolve systems. In addition, the Federal Government requires connectivity between multiple processing environments and applications operating on a variety of technology platforms

Implications: The Federal Government should adopt open system standards in which the interrelationships of components are fully defined by interface standards available to the public and maintained by group consensus. The Federal Government should adopt, acquire, and integrate those components that conform to specification. An open system architecture is the goal; however, initially only partially open systems will be attained. This principle could lead to use of JAVA and future JAVA-like protocols, which give a high priority to platform independence. The Federal Government should be able to ensure compliance with these standards.

2. **Investments** *Coordinate technology investments with the Federal business and architecture.*

Rationale : The completed current architecture, or a portion of it, should be considered the baseline or the starting point for optimization. Optimization will occur over time and investments made consistent with the business needs (i.e., over individual needs) and incorporated into the architecture. It is important to define the current and target positions and identify those investments in the architecture that will achieve the target position.

Implications : Compliance mechanisms are necessary to ensure that investments are funded by business and architectural decisions and consistently align the architecture with business needs. This alignment applies to multiagency and Governmentwide investments, as well as Agency and Bureau investments to achieve vertical integration. Technology advances are welcome, and the technology blueprint can change when compatibility with the current infrastructure, improvement in operational efficiency, or a required capability is demonstrated.

3. **Data Collection** *Minimize the data collection burden.*

Rationale: The Federal Government should be able to collect, manipulate, and transmit accurate and consistent data quickly and easily. The lack of data integration due to incompatible database structures; poor quality and integrity of data; and the mixture of organizations, processes, and business rules with data, hinder data collection, manipulation, and transmission. Data should be shared across the Federal Government.

Implications: Data standardization, including a common vocabulary and data definition, will be difficult to achieve but is critical. A common organization eliminates redundancy and ensures data consistency. To ensure success, business units as well as IT personnel should be involved. Each data element should have a trustee accountable for data quality.

4. **Security** *Secure Federal information against unauthorized access.*

Rationale : The Federal Government must be aware of security breaches and data compromise and the impact of these events. Appropriate security monitoring and planning, including an analysis of risks and contingencies and the implementation of appropriate contingency plans must be completed to prevent unauthorized access to Federal information. Information security must be ensured and increased, commensurate with increased access to Federal information.

Implications : Protecting systems from spies, terrorists, and hackers requires considerable effort and costs. The business unit manager, where each system is implemented, must take responsibility for security measures and contingency plans as required by Presidential Decision Directive-63 (PDD-63), *Critical Infrastructure Protection.*

5. **Functionality***: Take advantage of standardization based on common functions and* *customers.*

Rationale: Due to a lack of standardization on common functions and customers, Federal Agencies have not taken advantage of reuse or incorporated commercial products into Federal systems. Applications have not been developed using standard system components shared across the organization. Additionally, similar or duplicative applications have been developed.

Implications: Federal Agencies should develop or design reusable components or purchase architecture components, recognizing that these items are designed to obtain a particular functionality. Increasingly, the Federal Government is becoming a consumer as opposed to the producer of components; this role requires new skills and abilities. Standardization on common functions and customers will help Federal Agencies implement change in a timely manner. For commercial and Government-off-the-Shelf (GOTS) software applications, current choices may be limited, as many of these applications are technology and platform dependent.

*6. **Information Access**: Provide access to information.*

Rationale: In accordance with the Paperwork Reduction Act (PRA, PL 104-13), the Federal employee and the public should have access to Government information efficiently, effectively, and economically. The right information should be attainable any place, any time, and in the right format.

Implications: The Federal Government should encourage a diversity of public and private access methods for Government public information, including multiple access points, the separation of transactional from analytical data, and data warehousing architecture. Accessibility involves the ease with which users obtain information. Information access and display must be sufficiently adaptable to a wide range of users and access methods, including formats accessible to those with sensory disabilities.

*7. **Proven Technologies** Select and implement proven market technologies.*

Rationale: Federal Agencies often concentrate attention on "bleeding edge" technology, which results in wasted time and effort. The Federal Enterprise Architecture should focus on proven market technologies implemented within a reasonable period. Business flexibility has been lost and the Government has not adjusted quickly to change. Unfortunately, the environment is often a tangled web of systems, making implementation of proven market technology difficult.

Implications: Systems should be developed based on global data classes and process boundaries. Systems should be decoupled to allow maximum flexibility. Incorporating new or proven technology in a timely manner will help Agencies to cope with change.

*8. **Privacy** Comply with the Privacy Act of 1974.*

Rationale: Federal Agencies should know and apply the principles of the Privacy Act of 1974 and incorporate them into investments.

Implications: A privacy notice that includes the purpose for the information request should be provided anytime the public provides or enters data. The public should be given the right to choose whether or not to provide information. When information is used for other purposes or those other than originally intended, an alternative privacy notice should be provided. Again, the public should be allowed to choose whether or not to provide the information. Protecting the privacy of the citizen is a tremendous burden and management must consider the potential uses of information. In addition, privacy information maintained by the Government will be properly secured.

Index

A

Accessibility, information technology, 142–143
Acquisition life cycle, 78, 80, 82
Acronyms, 133–134
Across-the-board marginal funding, 101
Adaptability, 20, 21
Advertising, 77
  push, 135
Agile enterprise
  characterization, 16–18
  best-practice enterprise architecture, 74
    external relationships management, 109
    human resources management, 96
    improvement/change management, 110, 111, 112
  implementing best-practice enterprise
    current initiatives/relationships, 121–122
    learning organization, 128, 129
    robust enterprise components and flexible architecture, 127
  goals of totally integrated enterprise, 15
  process view, 57
  robust components reusability, 21
Agility, 16–18, *see also* Agile enterprise
Alliances, 109
American Productivity & Quality Center (AP&QC)
  best-practice enterprise architecture, 69

classification framework and enterprise assessment, 176
rights and permissions, 152–159
API, *see* Application programming interfaces
Application architecture, 64
Application programming interfaces (API), 164, 165, 166, *see also* Interfaces
Architectural models, 189
Architectural progression, 59–62
Architectural requirements, 24
Architectural segments, 189
Archive, 144
Audible control mechanisms, 102
Automobile manufacturer, 119–120
Autonomous function, 135
Autonomy, 20, 21

B

Backup, 144
Balance, 12, 50
Benchmarking, 135
Best-practice enterprise, implementation
  case studies, 119–121
  current initiatives and relationships, 121–122
  innovation trends, 130–132
  integrated product management, 123–125
  learning organizations, 128–130

195

S

Safety issues, 105
Salary, 96
Scalability, 14, 20
Scales of economy, 57
Scope creep, 15
Security, 127, 147, 191
Segment approach, 188, *see also* Federal
      enterprise architecture
      framework
Selection, information technology, 149
Shared-creation-for-value enterprise, 32
Shared objectives, 14
Shared processes, 137
Shareholder, 72
Simplicity, enterprise, 50
Simulations
    best-practice enterprise architecture, 89,
      92–93
    component-based enterprise and robust
      components, 22
    definition, 137
    goals of totally integrated enterprise, 16
    process view of enterprise, 57
Skill, 21
Software tools, 42
Special-interest groups, 103
Stability, 19
Standardization, 126
Standards, 91, 170, 189, 190
State-of-the-art, enterprise, 74, 76
Status quo approach, 188, *see also* Federal
      enterprise architecture
      framework
Stockholders, 107
Strategic direction, 61, 189
Strategies
    best-practice enterprise architecture, 70,
      72–73, 90
    framework for integrated enterprise, 47,
      49
Structural architecture, 4
Structured decomposition, 22
Subarchitectures, 171
Subcontracting, 11, 12, 109
Summary component, 22
Supplier, 109
Support/enabling
    best-practice enterprise architecture, 69

    customer acquisition process, 90
    efficiencies, 94–95
    product development process, 91–92
    best-practice enterprise implementation,
      124, 125, 129
    information technology, 147–148
Survivability, 14, 16, 17
Survivable systems, 127
System provider, 10–11, 12
Systems-level view, 104, 105

T

Taguchi methods, 91
Target architecture, 189
Target markets, 87
Tax regulations, 105
Taxonomy, 5, 87
Teaming, 30
Technology, development, 111
Technology architecture, 64, *see also*
      Federal enterprise architecture
      framework
TIE, *see* Totally integrated enterprise
Tier one suppliers, 11–12
Tier two suppliers, 12
Tools, 56, 58, 177, 179
Total quality management (TQM), 112–113
Totally integrated enterprise (TIE)
    agility, 16–18
    collaborative, 31–33
    component-based, 22–25
    definition and scope of architecture, 3–6
    goals, 10–16
    integrated product teams, 29–31
    robust components, 18–22
    value-based, 25–27
    virtual capability, 27–29
TQM, *see* Total quality management
Transitional processes, 189
Triangular model, 46

U

Unique processes, 60, 137
U-shaped patterns, assembly lines, 102